An Introduction
to
INDIAN MUSIC

B. CHAITANYA DEVA

PUBLICATIONS DIVISION
MINISTRY OF INFORMATION AND BROADCASTING
GOVERNMENT OF INDIA

First Edition: 1973 (*Magha 1894*)
Fourth Revised Edition : 2015 (*Saka 1937*)

© Publications Division

ISBN - 978-81-230-1999-4
A&C-ENG-REP-004-2015-16

Price : ₹ 175.00

Published by Additional Director General,
Publications Division, Ministry of Information and Broadcasting,
Government of India, Soochna Bhawan,
CGO Complex, Lodhi Road, New Delhi-110003

http://www.publicationsdivision.nic.in

Editing : Shyamala. M. Iyer
Cover Design : Asha Saxena
Photo Page Layout: Gajanan. P. Dhope

Sales Centres : • Soochna Bhavan, C.G.O. Complex, Lodhi Road, **New Delhi**-110003
• Hall No. 196, Old Secretariat, **Delhi**-110054 • 701, B-Wing, Kendriya Sadan,
Belapur, **Navi Mumbai**-400614 • 8, Esplanade East, **Kolkata**-700069 • 'A' Wing,
Rajaji Bhawan, Besant Nagar, **Chennai**-600090 • Press Road, Near Govt. Press,
Thiruvananthapuram-695001 • Block 4, 1st Floor, Gruhakalpa Complex, M.G. Road,
Nampally **Hyderabad**-500001 • 1st Floor, 'F' Wing, Kendriya Sadan, Koramangala,
Bangaluru-560034 • Bihar State Co-operative Bank Building, Ashoka Rajpath, **Patna**-
800004 • Hall No. 1, 2nd Floor, Kendriya Bhawan, Sector H, Aliganj, **Lucknow**-
226024 • Ambica Complex, 1st Floor, Paldi, **Ahmedabad**-380007 • House No. 7, New
Colony, Cheni Kuthi, KKB Road **Guwahati**-781003.

Typesetter : Quick Prints, Naraina, New Delhi-110 028.
Printed at : J. K. Offset Graphics Pvt. Ltd. O.I.A., Phase-1, New Delhi-110 020

To
SINDHU
my wife

PREFACE

There are quite a number of books on Indian music, a few of them excellent. Some are highly technical, of interest only to the specialists; some, though simpler, are out dated. A few have restricted themselves either to the Northern or the Southern system of classical music. An attempt has been made here, therefore, to present an introduction to our music in a comprehensive but simple manner. While this volume is not a learned tome, neither is it a bedside book, much less a tourist guide. Certain amount of earnestness and interest are expected of the reader. Also the book is intended both for Indian and foreign friends. It may even interest a specialist, because of its analytical methods.

The approach throughout has been: go from the known to the unknown. Hence current musical practice is always given prominence; for this is the only music one can hear, appreciate and understand. The historical material goes only to give a backdrop against which the present art can get a perspective. So, history has a secondary place here. Even there, I have tried to relate music to the larger social dynamics of Indian culture.

The historical process of cultural development has given us two systems of sophisticated music: the North Indian (Hindustani) and the South Indian Carnatic. Whether these two resulted from the bifurcation of a more ancient single 'Indian' music or are the consequence of fusion of regional styles is a question that need not be discussed here. But both are 'Indian', howsoever one may define that word; they have a high degree of commonness, though quite clearly distinctive also. Hindustani music is performed and understood throughout North India and the Northern district of Karnataka and Andhra; Carnatic music is confined to the Southern peninsula. The present book treats both together, though not necessarily as 'one' music.

The reader may recognize two sections: the grammatical and the socio-historical. The first is a description of the structure of Indian music; this analyses the *raga*, the *tala*, the *prabandha* and so on. It helps the reader-listener to understand the actual way of the construction of the music. The second part is the socio-historical background and the aesthetics of Indian music. This gives the necessary orientation and viewpoint required for the appreciation of this art.

True understanding is always a total comprehension which is different from synthesis. The latter implies putting together things which are different; but understanding is total immediate perception which cannot be communicated by 'words' and 'notes'. So analytical has the modern mind become, that it has entailed a 'guide to listening'. To many a Westerner, Indian music may be a melody without a specific beginning or a definite end. To many Indians it is more a gymnastics in sound. A help to listen has, therefore, to be provided sometimes. This book is an attempt to introduce mainly the classical music of India to both kinds of listeners who are earnest but find the technicalities a little baffling.

The best beginning is to listen to, and if possible, produce the music. The second may not be possible to all. But with modern adjuncts like the gramaphone, the radio and the tape-recorder it is always possible to hear music. To assist the reader, therefore, a discography and also a small bibliography are added at the end; the author is grateful to Shri O. Varkey, Librarian, Sangeet Natak Akademi, New Delhi, for assistance in the preparation of these, from the material available in their archives.

New Delhi, 1973   B.C. DEVA

CONTENTS

1

Introduction

THE WORD for music now used in India is *sangeeta*. There is, however, a slight mistranslation here. For *sangeeta* in its original or more traditional usage did not mean music but a comprehensive 'performing art' of singing, playing of instruments and dancing. Moreover, the art was generally a part of drama, and even Bharata, the earliest writer on dramaturgy, had only a few chapters on music in his great treatise, *Natyasastra*. Notice, again, the great respect to vocal music–for *sangeeta* had *geeta* (singing) as its main limb followed by instrumental music and then by dancing.

Once upon a time, a king, desirous of learning sculpture, went to a learned sage and asked to be taught the art. But the teacher said, "How can you know the laws of sculpture, if you do not know painting?". Teach me the art of painting, Master", said the disciple. "But how will you understand painting, without the knowledge of dance?" "Instruct me in the techniques of dance, O Wise One", requested the royal student. The teacher continued, "But you cannot dance without knowing instrumental music". "Let me learn the laws of instruments", prayed the king. The *guru* replied, "Instrumental music can be learnt only if you study deeply the art of singing". If singing is the fountain head of all arts, I beg you, O Master, to reveal to me the secrets of vocal music". This prime place given to the voice in ancient times still abides and many of the qualities of Indian music derive their characteristics from this fact.

The music of India is essentially melodic. Whether it be the yell of the most primitive tribes or the sophisticated art form, whether it is vocal or instrumental, the music is 'linear'. Sounds follow one another expressing an emotional state and an aesthetic unity; they are not sounded simultaneously, which is harmony. Not that harmony is absent, but it is an incipient condition and has not been developed to the extent as in the West. Tonal qualities and colours do clash creating grades of consonance and dissonance. The melodic form may be just a monotone (a song sung in a single note) as in the songs of corn grinding, a grunt of an expletive of the

Nagas, a chant of the Vedic hymn or a most complicated *raga*. A humble tune of the roadside snake charmer may even be developed into *raga Punnagavarali*. But basically all these are 'tunes', that is, an up and down of sound with a certain sense of rhythm and emotional appeal.

This rise and fall of tones has a certain accent in time or time division. This is the simplest meaning of the rhythm of a song. In a primitive stage this rhythm is a bodily activity of stamping and clapping which are developed and stylised into the complicated system of the 108 *talas* of classical music.

Thus in the study of our music the two major ideas or 'terms' which have to be understood are : (a) the structure of melody and (b) the structure of rhythm.

Melodic structure involves various questions such as: How does the sound rise and fall? Are the rise and fall linear or meandering? Are there 'areas' of a melody or *raga* which find more emphasis than others and so on. These and other aspects become the technical points of the grammar of *raga*.

Similarly, rhythmic organization comprise facets like: How is time divided? What is the meaning of tempo? How are the divisions of time arranged? Do these arrangements make for patterns? How does rhythm control melody?" Such queries form the basis of the grammar of *tala*.

Of course, what has been said above is only about the technicalities of music. But a land which has had millennia of civilization, a fantastic variety of culture and geographic distribution of great immensity presents a multitude of social and cultural problems related to music. A study of these gives the necessary background for understanding the present. So the history, social relations, aesthetic attitude and such matters will have to be discussed.

At the foundation of the music of any land is the 'unsophisticated' art of the people–the folk music. For it is out of this matrix, which often is undistinguishable from mere expletives in the most primeval state, has grown the art music of the 'civilized'. Moreover, music at this level is functional, unlike in the society of the 'leisured' class. It is an integral part of the various social activities. Therefore, it gives us many clues to the socio-economic and the religious lives of the people.

One of the most interesting and informative aspects is the part played by musical instruments. Just as the 'invention' of a manual tool must have changed the life of man, the 'invention' of a musical instrument must have changed the music of man. It has affected (and has been affected by) vocal music. It has made possible the development of a musical theory. Also, of great significance is the study of migration of musical instruments, as, if one follows the routes of their travel, one becomes aware of the movements of human civilizations.

This migration and mixing of cultures is of particular interest for this peninsula. On the plains and mountains of this land have lived and died many a tribe and culture, each contributing its own, to the music of India. The interaction of these musical styles, indigenous and foreign, has resulted in the two broad systems of classical music–North Indian (Hindustani) and South Indian (Carnatic). They are similar to the extent of being melodic and having the same general concepts of *raga* and *tala*. But there are also differences–major and minor–that still distinguish them very clearly. With the coming of quicker and wider means of communication, the two are coming closer; stylistic characteristics, *ragas* and attitudes are being exchanged. Western influences are gaining ground, as did mid-western music some centuries ago. All this may result in a music of a different mould in the future. Even more far reaching in effect is industrial technology and the consequent urbanization, again an import from the West: not necessarily a 'great leap' in a 'forward' direction, though there have been salutary effects. These may yet give Indian music a new direction. But none knows what is in the womb of time and it would not be proper to speculate vaguely on the future music of India.

2

The First Term–Melody

INDIAN MUSIC, as already emphasized, is essentially melodic. The music of the folks and tribes, of religious and sacramental chant and classical art music–all these have the common quality of being based on melody, and ages of experimentation and artistic development of these have given us the concept of *raga* which is the fundamental basis of Indian musical tradition.

The *raga* is a melodic-scheme. It is a nucleus based on certain traditionally accepted rules which in actual performance are improvised upon, expanded and embellished, thus drawing out the possibilities inherent in the melodic embryo. This simple idea has been made unnecessarily complicated by the pedant. Our music having grown almost totally on the lines of melody, has produced vast varieties of such types of tunes with very subtle differences and it requires an intimate acquaintance with its range to grasp the significance of these subtleties. But the concept of *raga* itself is straightforward and not difficult to understand.

To know what a *raga* is, it is best to start with the analogy of language and speech. This is not a far-fetched comparison, for the simple reason that speech and music are both communicative processes. Of course, what is communicated by speech cannot or need not be the same as what is communicated by music. But the obvious fact is that music does communicate something–even if it is a 'mood'.

Speech is actual sound–spoken and heard. But a language is an abstraction: a concept which is derived from speech. If one examines this question more closely, one will see that speech is first and fundamentally a flow of sound. Various kinds of tones produced and heard are designated as vowels and consonants, and these are put together as words forming a language. The visual representation of these speech-sounds is the orthography–for example, the printed letter which you are reading.

Analogously, a melody is a flow of sound—up and down, with various rhythmic distributions. When we abstract these characteristics and make a 'type', it becomes a '*raga*'–a musical 'language'. Here again, out of a stream of sound, 'notes' are created and named, and a particular arrangement of these 'notes' becomes a *raga*. The visual representation of such musical symbols is the notation.

Thus there is a general similarity between language and *raga*. This parallelism is a loose one and the analogy cannot be too strict. For instance, while there is a considerable degree of freedom in the succession of notes in *raga*, one cannot spell a word or construct a sentence with the same lack of consideration for linguistic grammar.

A *raga*, then, may be defined broadly as a melodic scheme, characterised by a definite scale or notes (alphabet), order of sequence of these notes (spelling and syntax), melodic phrases (words and sentences), pauses and stases (punctuation) and tonal graces (accent). Of course, there is always a rider attached to this: a *raga* must be pleasing; it must have emotional appeal. Therefore, an ancient definition runs, "A *raga*, the sages say, is a particular form of sound which is adorned with notes and melodic phrases and enchants the hearts of men". As a matter of fact, the word *raga* is derived from the root *ranj* (Sanskrit), to please. Further, its general lexical meaning is also 'emotion', 'colour' and so on.

We shall now turn to the grammar of *raga*.

The alphabet

The vowels and consonants in speech differ from one another by sound qualities and a group of such vocal sounds becomes the alphabet of a language. In music, by analogy, we have a set of musical sounds called notes or *svaras*. (A *svara* is not strictly a static phenomenon; but we shall not enter into that discussion now.) One *svara* is different from one another by being 'higher' or 'lower'. That is, *svara* differ from one another in pitch.

There are two kinds of alphabets in music. One is the basic collection of notes obtaining in music in general. These are the seven major *svaras* known as *Shadja, Rishabha, Gandhara, Madhyama, Panchama, Dhaivata* and *Nishada*, for short, shown as *Sa, Ri, Ga, Ma, Pa, Dha*, and *Ni*.

In this group each *svara* is 'higher' (greater in pitch) than the previous one. The difference in pitch between two consecutive notes in the above series—that is, the *interval* between them—is very distinct and distinguishable. It is possible, therefore, to interpolate another note between any adjacent ones. Thus, there can be intermediate notes between the following pairs: *Sa-Ri, Ri-Ga, Ga-Ma, Ma-Pa, Pa-Dha, Dha-Ni* and *Ni-Sa*.

To distinguish the new *svaras* and the 'original' or standard notes, two words are used: *suddha* and *vikrita*. *Suddha svaras* (natural notes) are the seven given first. *Vikrita svaras* are the intervening ones. We, then, have *vikrita rishabha* (between *Sa* and *Ri*), *vikrita gandhara* (between *Ri* and *Ga*), *vikrita madhyama* between (*Ma* and *Pa*), *Vikrita dhaivata* (between *Pa* and *dha*) and *Vikrita nishada* (between *Dha* and *Ni*). These *vikrita* notes may be represented by the symbols *ri, ga, ma, dha* and *ni*. There are thus, in all twelve notes in the generalized musical alphabet arranged as under:

Sa Ri Ga Ma Pa Dha Ni   — *suddha svaras*

ri ga   ma   dha ni   — *vikrita svaras*

The reader may observe that there are no *vikrita* notes between *Ga* and *Ma, Ni* and *Sa*. This is so, because it is felt that these note-pairs are musically too close to tolerate an interpolation. If any *svara* is brought in between, say *Ga* and *Ma,* it is difficult to distinguish it from either of the above two. Similar is the case with the interval, *Ni-sa.* (These twelve *svaras* have been discussed in detail in the chapter on musical scales.)

In Western musical terminology these are the natural (7) notes and variants (5). Writing them in tonic sol-fa notation they can be arranged thus:

doh ray me fal soh lah te   — natural scale
d   r   m   f   s   l   t   — symbol for natural scale
     ra   ma fa la ta   — flats and sharp
In the scale of C these will be written as:

C   D   E   F   G   A   B

D*b*   E*b*   F#   A*b*   B*b*

Summarizing we have:

Indian name*	Tonic sol-fa	Key of C
Shadja (Sa)	do	C
Vikrita rishabha (ri)	ra	D*b*
Rishabha (Ri)	r	D
Vikrita gandhara (ga)	ma	E*b*
Gandhara (Ga)	m	E

* These names have variations in the two systems of our music and the above scheme follows the Hindustani music to a large extent; but we shall discuss this later on. All examples of music from now on will be in the scale of C.

Madhyama (Ma)	f	**F**
Vikrita madhyama (ma)	fe	**F#**
Panchama (Pa)	s	**G**
Vikrita dhaivata (dha)	la	**Ab**
Dhaivata (Dha)	I	**A**
Vikrita nishada (ni)	ta	**Bb**
Nishada (Ni)	t	**B**

A rough, though musically not very satisfying, idea of these can be got by playing either the harmonium or the piano (key of C). The notes are as shown here:

Fig. 2.1

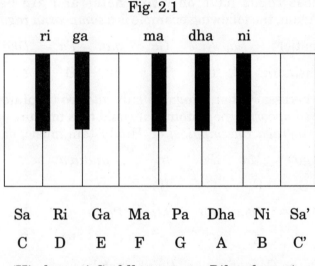

(Hindustani Suddha svara-s: Bilaval raga)

Though you are being advised to try the notes and various examples on a harmonium or a piano, you are also warned that Indian music, in its true form, cannot accept these instruments as correct. However, this simple aid will give a preliminary introduction to the musical material instanced.

What we listed above were the principal or generalized alphabet for Indian music as a whole. But a given *raga* does not, as a rule, have all the twelve notes. As a matter of fact, the use of twelve notes in a *raga* is rare. A few of these are selected and a *raga* employs only these chosen ones. Hence, we may say that every *raga* has its own alphabet of notes, which it neither exceeds nor reduces. Therefore, *ragas* are divided into various *jatis* (types) depending on the number of notes they have. For example, the simplest types are the *auduva* (five notes, pentatonic), *shadava* (six notes), hexatonic) *sampoorna* (seven notes, heptatonic).

As instances are the common *ragas Bhoopali* and *Malkaus* of Hindustani music (roughly corresponding to *Mohana* and *Hindola* of the Carnatic system). They use notes as shown:

Bhoopali :	Sa	Ri,	Ga,	Pa	Dha
	C	D	E	G	A
Malkaus :	Sa,	ga,	Ma,	dha,	ni
	C,	Eb,	F,	Ab,	Bb

Both these *ragas* have only five notes and are hence *auduva* (pentatonic). Again, the following example is a *sampoorna raga* (heptatonic):

Kalyani (Carnatic) :	Sa,	Ri,	Ga,	ma,	Pa,	Dha,	Ni
Yaman (Hindustani):	C,	D,	E,	F#,	G,	A,	B

It is not necessary that a *raga* be only *auduva* (pentatonic), *shadava* (hexatonic) or *sampoorna* (heptatonic): it could be a mixture of any of these For example, the *raga Bheempalasi* of Hindustani music, has:

Ascent:	Sa	ga	Ma	Pa	ni	—auduva
	C	Eb	F	G	Bb	

Descent :	Sa' ni	Dha	Pa	Ma	Pa	ga	Ma	ga	Ri
	C Bb	A	G	F	G	Eb	F	Eb	D

Similarly the Carnatic *raga Balahamsa* has:

Ascent :	Sa Ri	Ma	Pa	Dha
	C D	F	G	A

Descent :	Sa' ni	Dha	Pa	Ma	Ri;	Ma	Ga
	C' Bb	A	G	F	D	F	E

Both these are *auduva-sampoorna* (pentatonic-heptatonic)

Similarly we have the following *shadava-sampoorna: Kambhoji* (Carnatic):

Ascent :	Sa	Ri	Ga	Ma	Pa	Dha
	C	D	E	F	G	A

Descent: *Sa ni   Dha   Pa   Ma   Ga   Ri*

     C'   B♭   A   G   F   E   D

It is possible to show, by a simple arithmetical working, the total number of such possible combination of ascents and descents; and based only on the number of notes used in the ascent-descent combinations there can be 483 *ragas*.

In delineating a *raga* a musician will ordinarily not use a *svara* not proper to it i.e., not in its alphabet. For instance, *ri, ga, Ma, ma, dha, ni* and *Ni* cannot be employed in the *raga Bhoopali (Carnatic Mohana)*. Such notes that are omitted are called *varja svaras*. However, sometimes an alien note does creep in as an accidental, but intentional, *svara* for purposes of artistic beauty. But this introduction of a note foreign to the *raga* requires great skill, if the mood and structure of melody are not to be spoilt.

Musical Syntax and Spelling

Now it is not possible to define a language only by its alphabet. Two languages say, English and French (barring a few accents), Hindi and Marathi, Kannada and Telugu, may have the same set of letters, but the rules of combining them are very different and this is one of the distinctions in such language pairs.

There is a similar difference between *ragas* using the same notes. But they have different orders of their arrangement and there are certain rules accepted traditionally which insist on certain ways of melodic ascent and descent. The ascent is called *arohana* and the descent *avarohana*.

Consider a set of notes as:

Sa,   Ri,   ga,   Ma,   Pa,   dha,   ni

C,   D,   E♭,   F,   G,   A♭,   B♭

These can be ordered or spelt in various ways. For example, we can have the following two progressions while ascending in a melody:

1. *Sa,   Ri,   Ma,   Pa,   dha*

    C,   D,   F,   G,   A♭

2. *Sa,   Ri,   ga,   Ma,   Pa,   dha,   ni*

    C,   D,   E♭ F,   G,   A♭,   B♭

The two are musically different and, therefore, can form the syntax of different *ragas*. This is actually so. The first order is used in *Jaunpuri* and the second in *Darbari Kanada* (both of the Hindustani system).

While descending a variety of ways is possible:

1.   *Sa, ni,   dha, Pa,   Ma,   ga,   Ri*

     C,   B*b*,   A*b*, G,   F   E*b*,   D

2.   *Sa, dha, ni,   Pa,   ga,   Ma,   Ri*

     C,   A*b*, B*b*, G   E*b*   F,   D

Raga Jaunpuri used the first descent and *Darbari Kanada* the second. Thus, *Jaunpuri* will ascend and descend as follows:

Sa, Ri, Ma, Pa, dha, /   Sa' ni   dha Pa Ma   ga   Ri

C   D   F   G   Ab   /   C'   Bb   Ab   G   F   Eb   D

No phrase in this *raga* can be rendered in any other manner. For instance, a progression like *Sa, Ri, ga, Ma* (C D E*b* F) is wrong, for according to the rule just noted, *ga* (E*b*) cannot be taken in the ascending section of this *raga*.

This kind of difference obviously introduces another factor of uniqueness of melodic form. The ascent (*arohana*) and descent (*avarohana*) may or may not be the same. As examples we may take *ragas Mohana* and *Jaunpuri*. The former has the same five notes both in going up and coming down the scale. Not so the other *raga*. It has five notes permissible in *arohana* but seven in *avarohana*. Therefore, *Mohana* is, an *auduva-auduva raga* (pentatonic-pentatonic) and *Jaunpuri* an *auduva–sampoorna raga* (pentatonic-heptatonic).

Now look back at the decent of *raga Darbari Kanada* and compare it with *Jaunpuri*. The latter had a straight descent down the scale. But the former comes down in a very tortuous manner, though using all the seven notes. Such a movement is called *vakra sanchara* (crooked movement). The *raga* has therefore a *sampoorna vakra avarohana*—heptatonic crooked movement.

Notice again the *ragas Bheempalasi* and *Balahamsa* mentioned earlier. Both have crooked descents *only in parts*. In both the upper tetrachords are straight; but the lower tetrachord is *vakra*. In *Bheepalasi*, the twist is at *ga* (E*b)*; instead of going down as *Ma Ga Ri Sa* (F E D C) the movement (*sanchara)* chooses to turn upwards from *ga* (E*b*) and then flows down. The reader would like to analyse *Balahamsa* on similar lines. Sometimes, even the *svaras* may be different in ascent and descent. A common *raga* of such a structure is *Khamaj* wherein may be noted the *Ni* in *arohana* and *ni* in *avarohana*, thus:

Sa Ga Ma Pa Dha Ni / Sa' ni   Dha   Pa Ma Ga Ri

C E F G A B / C' Bb   A   G   F   E   D

(This *raga* will be *shadava-sampurna*; hexatonic-heptatonic). Naturally, the possibilities of such combinations are enormous.

Melodic Phrase

Besides the notes and their order, there are certain characteristic phrases always occurring in a *raga* which give it its melodic form. They have to be repeated and emphasized, so that the uniqueness of the *raga* is made clear. Such phrases are called *pakad, anga, varna, ranjana svara* (the catch phrase, a part, a movement, the phrase that catches the mind). For instance, a very common one is *ga Ma Ri (Eb* F D). This is peculiar (though not unique) to the *Kanada* group of *ragas*. If you hear this melodic sequence anywhere, you can be almost sure that some form of *Kanada raga* is being sung or played. (This line of notes is also found in *ragas* like *Malhar'*, *Bahar* and some others. But what has been said is a good rule of the thumb). The *anga* is like the physical personality of a human being. It is not just enough that organs and limbs are present. The uniqueness of the person is not in just having a set of arms, legs and a head, but in how they are placed in relation of another. So it is with a *raga*. It has one or more defining phrases which identify it and this is more than having a set of defined *svaras*. Hindustani musicians have a word for this separate identity—*shakal* (face). When there is a confusion in the pattern, they say, "The *shakal* (face) has not been drawn correctly".

Melodic Punctuation

Apart from syntax and phrasing, punctuation of melody is a very important aspect of a *raga*. Certain rules are accepted which prescribe the note to be emphasized, the note to be used at the beginning of a line, the note to end it with and so on. A knowledge and appreciation of this is necessary if one is to have insight into the construction of a *raga*. A wrong melodic beginning or a mistaken emphasis will not only ruin the mood of the music but may suggest another *raga*. It may do as much damage of the exposition of the *raga* as the wrong placement of a comma to the meaning of a sentence.

Vadi: This is the word designating the note most significant in a *raga* and which gives it a colour of its own. The word means "one that speaks". Being the most important note, it is called the "king of the *raga*". The music is so developed that this *svara* comes out prominent. It can be done by staying on it longer than on other notes, by constant repetition or building up musical idioms which emphasize it.

Samvadi is a note which has a relation of fourth or fifth (that is, it is a *Ma* or a *Pa*) to the *vadi* and constitutes a musical reflection or balance to *vadi*. It is the "*minister*". So when singing a *raga* the *samvadi* also should be made bold. Not only so, it holds a similar position in its melodic context as the *vadi* does.

Anuvadi svaras are those notes other than the *vadi* and *samvadi* in a *raga*. They are stressed or omitted to varying degrees and are subordinate in importance to the other two. They are, therefore, the servants in the kingdom of *raga*.

Vivadi svara is a dissonant note: it is the enemy and if used will destroy the mood of the melody.

These note types (*vadi, samvadi, anuvadi* and *vivadi*) provide the bases for melodic stases and punctuations. They thus determine to a large extent, the ethos as well as the structure of the *raga*. They are so important, particularly the *vadi*, that the same scale of notes can be made to yield different *ragas* by the mere change of *vadi* and hence, the *samvadi*. Listen for instance, to the *ragas Bhoopali* and *Deskar* (Hindustani). Both have the same set of *svaras, Sa Ri Ga Pa Dha* (C D E G A). But the former moves in such a way that Ga gets emphasis and the latter makes prominent *Dha*. Thus, the same scale forms different *ragas* with distinct moods by this simple expedient of change in *vadi*. It is worthwhile listening to *ragas Pooriya, Marva* and *Sohni* to grasp the significance of this point.

Besides these, there are recognized rules that prescribe the notes on which one can pause—the *nyasa svara*. Similarly, the note characteristically commencing a section of the melody is called the *graha* (that which is held). Often the change in the *nyasa* or *graha* will land a musician in another *raga*.

Accent and Intonation

A word or sentence is a concept in grammar and unpracticed speech; for example, when one starts learning to speak a language, it is more or less skeletal and does not have the typical native brogue, accent and intonation.

So also in a *raga*. A set of notes sung flat or in a staccato style has a limited appeal. To give a tone flesh and blood and to decorate it, has to be accented and intoned in such a manner that it gets an emotional content. This is achieved by attacking and releasing the sounds in various ways; by swinging, by gliding from one note to another and so on. These add great beauty to the music which otherwise would remain drab. Such nuances are known as *gamakas*. As they say, "When, in music, a note moves from its own pitch towards another so that the second sound passes like a shadow over it, this is called a *gamaka*." Again, "The grace that pleases the mind of the hearer is a *gamaka*".

Now, there can be literally an infinite number of *gamakas*. For there is no limit to the imagination and ingenuity of the musician. The sudden dips, touches and glides can be executed at various speeds and intensities which depend on virtuosity and creativity. By and large these embellishments come out almost unconsciously. However, there are some well recognized and consciously defined elements of beautification such as *tiripa* (flurry), *kampita* (shake), *meend* or *jaru* (glide) and *andolana* (swing).

It is not necessary that an artiste uses one or all of these during a performance—though he usually does. He even creates many more on the spot. Further, it is also important to note that the *gamaka* is not always definitive to a *raga*. That is, any *gamaka* can be employed in any *raga*. However, almost every *raga* has certain peculiar *gamakas* on some of its notes which are a *sine qua non*. For example, if you listen to *Darbari Kanada*, you can easily recognize the slow swinging of *ga* (E♭); or be on the look out for the touch of *Ma* (F) on Ga (E) in *Sankarabharana* (Carnatic system).

Melodic Patterns

The musical potentialities blossom out as the musician unfolds the *raga*. To do this, he will use not only its defining phrases and *gamakas* but a very important adjunct called *alankara, Alankara* literally means an ornament or a decoration. It is a repetitive musical pattern, in the sense that a given design is presented, as in embroidery. For instance, the following are two simple *alankaras:*

(Sa Ri Ga), Ri Ga Ma, Ga, Ma Pa

(C D E), D E F, E F G

(Sa Ri Ga Ri), Ri, Ga Ma Ga, Ga Ma Pa Ma

(C D E D), D E F E, E F G F

In each of the above the *design* of the notes in brackets is repeated.

The word *prastara* is used to mean elaboration in general. When a *raga* is being elaborated it is *raga prastara*. (When the intricacies of time are being shown it is *tala prastara* and so on.) Instrumentalists often call these kinds of progressions as *palta. Alankara* or patternment is one such *prastara*. Another very important method, used by the better trained musicians, is what is known as *khanda meru* or *svara prastara*, which is in essence a permutation and combination of notes. Take for instance, the three notes *Sa Ri Ga* (C D E), we can have the following *prastaras*:

Sa	Ri	Ga
Sa	Ga	Ri
Ri	Ga	Sa
Ri	Ga	Sa
Ga	Ri	Sa
Ga	Sa	Ri

and so on. If one had the time, patience and energy, one could work out the *khanda merus* for any number of notes in any *raga and* train oneself in them.

There are similar note exercises in Carnatic music and are called *varisai (varise, varusa)* which literally means alignment, arrangement, succession, etc. Some of the *varisai* are *sarali varisai* (linear arrangement), *janta varisai* (paired arrangement).

Eg. *Sarali Varisai:*

Sa ri Ga Ma, Sa ri Sa ri

Sa ri Ga Ma, Pa dha Ni Sa'

Janta varisai

Sa Sa ri ri / Ga Ga ri ri

Sa Sa ri ri / Ga Ga Ma Ma

There are, similarly, *datu varisai* which give patterns, wherein notes are in progression.

It will be noticed that these *varisais* have both tonal and rhythmic patterns, thus drilling the musician.

The *alankaras, khanda-merus, tanas* (see later) and *varaisai* are essentially scale exercises taught to students for voice and finger control as well as command over *raga* phrasealogy. But they always stand in good stead for *raga* elaboration.

To summarise:

Indian music, having grown on lines of melody, has developed the concept of *raga*. A *raga* is a melodic idea capable of elaboration and improvisation. The rules of grammar of a *raga* are:

1. It has a definite set of notes which are its alphabet.

2. The minimum number of notes for a *raga* is five and maximum nine. There are, however, exceptions.

3. It has a permitted manner of ascent (*arohana*) and descent (*avarohona*),

4. A *raga* uses characteristic melodic units (*pakad, chalan, tan, sanchara* or *varna*).

5. Certain *svaras* in its alphabet find emphasis to varying degrees (*vadi, sumvadi, anuvadi*). Melodic sections commence and end on defined notes (*graha* and *nyasa*).

6. While there are graces and accents common to all *ragas,* most of them have *gamakas* all their own, which give them distinctive qualities.

Every *raga,* then, is a melodic seed. Plant a seed in the soil; water it; manure it and husband it with love. The seed will grow into a fine tree with foliage, flowers and fruit. So with a *raga*; sow the melodic idea of a *raga* into the depths of the mind. Meditate on its potentialities and practise on its delicate revelations. Learn where and when to prune. It will grow into a beautiful musical form.

There are species of seeds. Each will give its own kind of plat: a mango seed will yield only a mango tree but not a banyan. However, no mango tree is identical with another mango tree. It is *essentially similar* but different in details, owing to the differences in the soil and environment. So with a *raga*. There are species and varieties of *ragas*. But each can expand only into its own form. However, no particular rendering of it is identical with any other. Two renderings of the same *raga* are *essentially similar*, but different in details owing to the temperament of the musician and the mood of the situation.

3

Genus and Species

IN THE STUDY of *ragas* we first laid down the alphabets of melody and recognized seven basic notes and five variations. These seven *svaras* (and the five variations) arranged in an order of increasing pitch form a scale or gamut, termed as *saptaka (sapta*—seven) in Indian music and an octave in the West. The arrangement is as under:

Indian Name	Signature	Sol-fa
Shadja	*Sa*	Doh
Rishabha	*Ri*	Re
Gandhara	*Ga*	Mi
Madhyama	*Ma*	Fa
Panchama	*Pa*	Sol
Dhaivata	*Dha*	La
Nishada	*Ni*	Ti

The eighth note (Sa^1) is a repetition of *Sa* and so one can have a series of *saptakas* with increasing pitches and a series of *saptakas* with decreasing pitches, thus:

. ... Ni_2 / $Sa_1 Ri_1 Ga_1 Ma_1 Pa_1 Dha_1 Ni_1$/Sa Ri Ga Ma Pa Dha Ni / $Sa^1 Ri^1$ ..

mandra sthayi (lower octave)	*madhya sthayi* (middle octave)	*tara sthayi* (upper octave)

If one sings in a natural voice, without strain, the pitch sung is taken to be *Sa*. From there one has to sing the other six notes *(Ri Ga Ma Pa Dha Ni)* to reach the higher *Sa,* shown as Sa^1. This is the *madhya saptaka.* Notes higher will be in progressively upper *saptakas.* Singing notes in the lower pitches will take us to lower octaves.

While *saptaka* is the word used to indicate a set of seven notes, another one, *sthayi,* is also current. This corresponds to 'register' in Western music.

The middle *saptaka is madhya sthayi,* the upper one *tara sthayi* and the lower one *mandra sthayi.* We can also have further higher octaves such as *ati tara sthayi* and lower ones like *anumandra sthayi.* The essential idea is a division of a continuum of pitches in sets of *saptakas* each extending from one *Sa* to another (the latter exclusive).

Again, in an earlier section we saw that besides these seven *svaras* there were another five interpolated variants or *vikrita svaras* making up in all twelve notes to an octave. These have different names in North Indian (Hindustani) and South Indian (Carnatic) music, as listed below :

Table 1

Hindustani	Carnatic	Sol-fa	Scale of C	Tone	Ratio	*Sruti*	Symbol
Shadja	*Shadjam*	Doh	C				*Sa*
Komal rishabh	*Suddha rishabham*		C#,D*b*	Major	9/8	4	*ri*
Suddha rishabh	*Chatussruti rishabham (Suddha gandharam)*	Re	D				*Ri*
Komal gandhar	*Sadharana gandharam (Shatsruti (rishabham)*		D#E*b*	Minor	10/9	3	*ga*
Suddha gandhar	*Antara gandharam*	Mi	E	Semi	16/15	2	*Ga*
Suddha madhyam	*Suddha madhyamam*	Fa	F				*Ma*
Teevra madhyam	*Prati madhyamam*		F#	Maj	9/8	4	*ma*
Pancham	*Panchamam*	Sol	G				*Pa*
Komal dhaivat	*Suddha dhaivatam*		G#, Ab				
Suddha dhaivat	*Chattussruti dhaivatam (Suddha nishadam)*	La	A	Maj	9/8	4	*dha* / *Dha*
Komal Nishad	*Kasiki nishadam (Shatsruti dhaivatam)*		A#, Bb,				*ni*
Suddha nishad	*Kakali nishadam*	Ti	B	Min	10/9	3	*Ni*
(Tara shadja)	*(Tara shadjam)*	Doh	C¹	Semi	16/15	2	*Sa'*

Note : If all the *srutis* are added from *Sa* to *Sa²* they will total up to 22. And if all the ratios are multiplied by one another they will give a product of 2. This is the measure of an octava or a *sthayi.*

One important adjective in the above list is *suddha* which means 'pure'. A Western musician would call this the 'natural'. The adjective qualifies the position of a note in a scale considered as standard and in terms of which other variants are compared. We shall, therefore, call this standard note and avoid the word *suddha*. There is another fact in the table which cannot escape our notice; the position of the *suddha* or standard *svara* in Hindustani and Carnatic music. In the former all standard notes, except *madhyama*, are higher than the *vikrita* which are qualified by the adjective *komal* (soft). In the other system, *suddha* is the lowest position and the variants are higher. However, there is one thing common, neither *Sa* (Doh) nor *Pa* (Sol) have any varieties; they are, therefore, called *achala* (immovable). So, writing down the standard scales we have:

Hindustani

Sa Ri Ga Ma Pa Dha Ni Sa¹ (Play the white keys on the harmonium).
C D E F G A B C¹

This is roughly the major scale of the West and is used in *raga Bilaval*.

Carnatic

Sa ri Ri Ma Pa dha Dha Sa¹ (Play the keys marked in Fig. 3.1).

C D*b* D F G Ab A C¹.

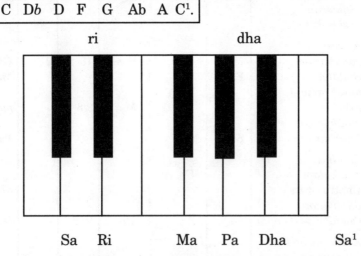

Fig. 3.1 : The *suddha svara-s* of Carnatic music.

Raga Kanakangi. In theory and in practice *Ri* and *Dha* are called *Ga* and *Ni*.

South Indian musicians will still call these as *Sa Ri Ga Ma Pa Dha Ni. Raga Kanakangi* employs these notes.

Before going to the classification of *ragas* on the basis of such scales, we may look into the matter of relations of *svaras* in the *saptakas,* as measured by *srutis* (microtones or 'quarter tones').

Sruti: The concept of *sruti* is the most significant but yet the most baffling aspect of Indian music and there are as many opinions as there are writers on the subject. For our present purposes, we shall understand a *sruti* to be a unit of measurement of the relation of notes in an octave. As a comparison, there are the semitones in Western music, twelve of them to an octave. Similarly, Indian music 'divides' a *saptaka (Sa* to *S^a)* into twenty-two intervals which are known as *srutis.* (These are not necessarily equal in size, like the tempered semitone; as a matter of fact, they are not). *Sruti* intervals between consecutive notes in a standard scale are shown in the table above; if all of them are added up they will total up to 22.

Are such fine intervals used in our music? Most definitely, yes. It is not exaggeration to say that the fineness of Indian music lies in the microdistinctions made in the pitches of *svaras.* For instance, the *komal rishabh* (Db) in *ragas Bhairavi, Pooriya* and *Bhairav* (all Hindustani) is different, the distinction lying in their *sruti* values. Even more important is the fact that a note alters its pitch by one or more *srutis,* depending upon whether it is employed in an ascending phrase or a descending one. Further, *gamakas* (graces) change the pitches of notes to delicate but perceptible extents. One has only to listen to *gandhara* (Eb) of *Todi* (Carnatic), *Darbari* (Hindustani), to experience this microtonal shades: what we call as 'distinctions of hairbreadth' *(kaisiki).* The term *sruti* has often found different definitions and explanations. For instance, Matanga (5th cent. A.D.) calls it 'a sound which can be grasped by the ear'. If we interpret this very broadly, we may say that any audible sound is *sruti.* Indeed, the word itself is derived from the root *sru*—to hear. Again an ancient author, Kohala, says that the number of *srutis* are infinite. But as an operational definition, we shall take it to be the just noticeable difference between two musical pitches.

Before closing this section, it will be useful to acquaint ourselves with some modern concepts of science in relation to ancient Indian ideas. In terms of current science, the pitch of a sound is generally expressed as the number of vibrations of the body producing the sound. And the relation between two pitches—the interval, as it is technically called—is shown as the ratio of the vibrations. Thus, if *Sa* is of 240 vibrations per second, *Ri* will be 270. Their ratio or interval is 270/240=9/8. This has been called an interval of four *srutis* in Indian music and major tone in Western music. Other such intervals have been shown in the Table 1

This leads to the question of what is known as 'absolute pitch'. Now, absolute pitch is an internationally standardized pitch; for instance, when a Western musician talks of A of the middle octave, he implies thereby a pitch of 440 vibrations per second. That is, a sound has an A-ness in a continuum of musical notes, irrespective of other pitches. This A-ness is, therefore, an absolute and not a relative characteristic. It is said that some people have the capacity to recognize this quality of the absolute pitches of sounds.

Indian music, however, does not conceive of such an absoluteness. Here, what is important is the relation of pitches. For instance, when a musician mentions *Dha* (La), he means a particular interval with a given sound as *Sa.* Any sound can be taken as *Sa,* and *Dha* is fixed only with reference to this sound. *Dha-ness* is thus only a relative value; it has no absolute standard. (Western readers will understand this as the difference between the absolute standard scales and the sol-fa system.) But some writers have tried to interpret an ancient verse as implying the existence of absolute pitch, at least in ancient music. This runs thus: "*Shadja* is uttered by the peacock and *Rishabha* by the *chataka* bird; the bleating of the goat is *Gandhara* and *Madhyama* by the heron; in the season of flowers (spring) the *cuckoo* signs the *Panchama;* during the rains the frog croaks *Dhaivata; Nishada* is trumpeted by the elephant in all seasons". Of course, this neither proves nor disproves anything.

Classification of Scales and Ragas

A set of seven *svaras,* chosen from the twelve, is a *mela* or *thata;* for purposes of *raga*-arrangement the words *saptaka* and *mela* are often interchangeable. But the former is more in the sense of measurement of an octave and the latter any octave of seven *svaras* for grouping *ragas*.

To put *ragas* into species, an octave is divided into two parts; these are *angas* equivalent to the two tetrachords of Western scale. The lower tetrachord is *poorvanga* and the upper one *uttaranga*. The first extends from *Sa* to *Pa* (C to G) and the second from *Ma* to *Sa* (F to C¹).

Consider the number of *poorvangas* possible, omitting *ma* (F#), the *anga* having four notes:

1.	*Sa*	*ri*	*Ri*	*Ma*	C	D♭	D	F
2.	*Sa*	*ri*	*ga*	*Ma*	C	D♭	E♭	F
3.	*Sa*	*ri*	*Ga*	*Ma*	C	D♭	E	F
4.	*Sa*	*Ri*	*ga*	*Ma*	C	D	E♭	F
5.	*Sa*	*Ri*	*Ga*	*Ma*	C	D	E	F
6.	*Sa*	*ga*	*Ga*	*Ma*	C	E♭	E	F

Similarly there can be six different *uttarangas* :

1.	Pa	dha	Dha	Sa	G	Ab	A	C
2.	Pa	dha	ni	Sa	G	Ab	Bb	C
3.	Pa	dha	Ni	Sa	G	Ab	B	C
4.	Pa	dha	ni	Sa	G	Ab	Bb	C
5.	Pa	Dha	Ni	Sa	G	A	B	C
6.	Pa	ni	Ni	Sa	G	Bb	B	C

Each of the *poorvangas* can be combined separately with every one of the *uttarangas,* giving thirty-six *melas* or *thatas.* For example, the first *poorvanga* can give, by different affixations, six scales as under:

Sa	ri	Ri	Ma	Pa	dha	Dha	Sa	C	Db	D	F	G	Ab	A	C*
Sa	ri	Ri	Ma	Pa	dha	ni	Sa	C	Db	D	F	G	Ab	Bb	C
Sa	ri	Ri	Ma	Pa	dha	Ni	Sa	C	Db	D	F	G	Ab	B	C
Sa	ri	Ri	Ma	Pa	Dha	ni	Sa	C	Db	D	F	G	A	Bb	C
Sa	ri	Ri	Ma	Pa	Dha	Ni	Sa	C	Db	D	F	G	A	B	C
Sa	ri	Ri	Ma	Pa	ni	Ni	Sa	C	Db	D	F	G	Bb	B	C

In all these cases the lower tetrachord *(poorvanga)* has been kept constant and the upper *(uttaranga)* varied. Similar combinations for other *angas* can be worked out.

So far all the *melas* had only the *Suddha Madhyama* (F). If this is substituted by *teevra madhyama* (F#), another set of thirty-six, differing only in the *madhyama* (Fourth) is obtained. In all therefore, there can be 72 basic scales or *melas,* and the first one marked* is the standard *(suddha)* in South India. It is the *mela* of *raga Kanakangi.*

This system was worked out to its logical conclusion by Venkatamakhi (17th cent.) for Carnatic music. Arithmetically so perfect was it that he exclaimed, "Even the Lord Creator can neither add nor reduce this number (72) by even one *mela*!". Certainly, it has been of great practical use to South Indian music.

The seventy-two scales are called *janaka melas* or *melakartas,* i.e., parent scales; and the *ragas* which employ these notes in straight ascent and descent are known as *janaka* or *karta ragas* (parent *ragas*). Further, a way of nomenclature, based on Sanskrit alphabetical order, has also been developed to identify the *janaka melas.* That is, each *mela* has been given a name and by working out the serial order of its spelling in Sanskrit, its number in the series of 72 can be found out. The adjective *janaka* is used because it generates other scales by omitting one or more notes, *Sa* and *Pa* (C and G) exempted. The rule is that *melas* 'born' by such deduction should never have less than four *svaras,* as any melody with less than this number of notes is not a *raga* but a mere tune. These derived scales are known as *janya melas;* that is, they are the progeny of the basic or parent gamuts (*janya*=born). The derived scale can be different in ascent and descent in a given *raga,* provided both of them are from the same parent. A further complication is introducing twists and turns in the ascent and descent of a *mela.* Theoretically, then, the number of derived scales can be astronomical in number and *ragas* infinite. In practice, however, not all of them are emotionally satisfying and hence only about 300 are known. Of these a hundred or so are common. A musician can, perhaps, render about fifty with some degree of confidence and some twenty-five with mastery. It is not easy to achieve a high degree of control over the complications of *raga,* to sing in perfect tune, with all qualifying *gamakas* and to introduce rhythmic variations but yet produce an aesthetically beautiful form, on the spot. Most artists are, therefore, known for their really fine grasp of half a dozen *ragas.* There is a story of a singer who was famous for his extraordinary control over the *raga Todi.* He would sing only this and none other, even at the royal court. But he was a pauper and owed much to a moneylender; unfortunately, he had no material valuable which he could pawn with the creditor. In desperation, the moneylender forced the musician to keep as a security his *raga Todi,* with the promise that he would not sing it till the loan was repaid in full. Next day the singer went to the royal court and the king ordered him to render *Todi.* The musician pleaded his inability and gave the reason as well. But the patron came up to the occasion. He paid the loan and freed the impoverished vocalist from the clutches of the creditor. Of course, what opinion he had about the musician, apart from his art, no one knows.

Current Hindustani system does not have such a comprehensive scheme of genus and species of scales and *ragas,* though the 72 *melas* or *thatas* are recognized for theoretical purposes. But considering the limited number used in actual practice and for certain theoretical reasons, only 36 are sometimes chosen. While this is useful to a large extent, there is yet another schedule—the Bhatkhande system—which has taken only ten *melas* or *thatas* as parents and these are named after the most popular *ragas* which use them. The ten *thatas* are :

Bilaval:	Sa	Ri	Ga	Ma	Pa	Dha Ni	C	D	E	F	G	A	B
Khamaj:	Sa	Ri	Ga	Ma	Pa	Dha ni	C	D	E	F	G	A	Bb
Kafi:	Sa	Ri	ga	Ma	Pa	Dha ni	C	D	Eb	F	G	A	Bb
Asavari:	Sa	Ri	ga	Ma	Pa	dha ni	C	D	Eb	F	G	Ab	Bb
Bhairav:	Sa	ri	Ga	Ma	Pa	dha Ni	C	Db	E	F	G	Ab	B
Bhairavi:	Sa	ri	ga	Ma	Pa	dha ni	C	Db	Eb	F	G	Ab	Bb
Kalyan:	Sa	Ri	Ga	ma	Pa	Dha Ni	C	D	E	F#	G	A	B
Marwa:	Sa	ri	Ga	ma	Pa	Dha Ni	C	Db	E	F#	G	A	B
Poorvi:	Sa	ri	Ga	ma	Pa	dha Ni	C	Db	E	F#	G	Ab	B
Todi:	Sa	ri	ga	ma	Pa	dha Ni	C	Db	Eb	F#	G	Ab	B

An attempt has been made to include all the known *ragas* into this scheme. In spite of a number of deficiencies—into which we need not enter here—this is the most popular system of classification in North India.

Evolution of Scales and Ragas

There are generally two sources from which melodies originate, mingle and react to evolve new ones. Tribal, folk and popular music form one area of origin. The art here is usually simple and there is little codification. The other is the ecclesiastical and sophisticated music which is commonly fitted into some kind of conscious grammar. There is always an interaction between all these various currents and the music of a culture comprises all these. Classical or art music in this country, while having its roots in folk music, has been dependent on the religious chant for the beginnings of its codification and we shall travel back nearly four thousand years to tap the earliest forms.

The music of the Indus Valley civilization which is generally supposed to be pre-vedic has not left any recorded evidence and it is only from the age of *Rigveda* (2500 B.C.) that we have been able to trace the sources of Indian musical grammar. The music of the Vedas was a kind of chant and the recitation had always a downward movement (starting from a high tone and ending on a normal pitch). The simplest chants were *archika* (single tone), and *gathika* (two-tone). The verse singing of later *Rigveda* had only three notes or regions of notes which were called *udatta, anudatta* and *svarita*. The first was the raised tone, the second was the grave and the third the middle tone. Roughly, these correspond to modern *Ri* (Re), *ni* (Ti flat) *Sa* (Doh). Eventually, this kind of chant grows into the singing of *Samaveda*. As a matter of fact, *Samaveda* is the musical version of *Rigveda*.

The hymns in both are textually the same; but while they are more or less recited in the latter, they are sung in the former. The scale of *Saman* chant is roughly, though not strictly, equivalent to the present day *Kafi* or *Kharaharapriya mela* (C D E*b* F GA B*b*).

A major landmark in musicology is the work, *Natyasastra,* of Bharata (2nd B.C.—4 A.D.). This book on dramaturgy has a few chapters on music and all later writers invariably go back to it for reference. Sage Bharata describes not one but *two* standard scales, *gramas. Grama* literally means a village or a gregarious habitation. By a transference of meaning, it had come to mean, in music, a group of notes. The two *gramas* were *shadja grama* and *madhyama grama,* and the distribution of intervals in the two were:

Shadja grama	Sa	Ri	Ga	Ma	Pa	Dha	Ni	Sa
Tones	Min	Semi	Maj	Maj	Min	Semi	Maj	
Srutis	3	2	4	4	3	2	4	
Madhyama grama								
Tones	Min	Semi	Maj	Min	Maj	Semi	Maj	
Srutis	3	2	4	3	4	2	4	

Another standard scale, *gandhara grama,* seems to have existed prior to Bharata. But by his time it had become obsolete, for Narada of 1st cent. A.D. says, "Three *gramas* are well known: *shadja, madhyama* and *gandhara; shadja grama* is in this world of humans, the *madhyama grama* in the nether world and the *gandhara grama* is in heaven and nowhere else."

Apart from the seven notes in each *grama,* two intercalary ones were known. They were: *antara gandhara* (E) between *gandhara* and *madhyama,* and *kakali nishada* (B) between *nishada* and *shadja,* of this ancient system.

The most important aspect of this stage of Indian music is the development of a large number of scales by what is called 'modal shift'. The term for this was *moorcchana* which means 'swooning'. Each note in a *grama* is taken as *Sa,* the succeeding notes becoming *Ni, Dha, Pa, Ma, Ga, Ri* in a descending order. It is because these new scales were produced by descent they were called *moorcchanas* (swooned or fallen). For example, taking only one *grama,* and that too without the intercalary notes, the following modal scales are possible:

Moorcchana														Name
2	4	4	3	2	4	3	2	4	4	3	2	4		*Srutis*
Ri	ga	Ma	Pa	Dha	ni	Sa	Ri	ga	Ma	Pa	Dha	ni	Sa	*Uttaramandra*
						S	R	G	M	P	D	N	S	*Rajani*
					S	R	G	M	P	D	N	S		*Uttarayata*
				S	R	G	M	P	D	N	S			*Suddhashadja*
			S	R	G	M	P	D	N	S				*Matsarikrta*
		S	R	G	M	P	D	N	S					*Asvakranta*
S	R	G	M	P	D	N	S							*Abhirudagata*

By this process notes of different intervals or *srutis* (major, minor and semi-tones) are obtained. Now, if we try the same process by introducing any one or both the intercalary notes (E and B), we get 32 *moorcchanas* from one *grama*. Since there are two *gramas,* there can be 64 scales. Thus our ancients had at least this number of scalic arrangements to organize their melodies in.

The easiest way to practically do this is on a harp or dulcimer. If you have a well tuned (modern) *veena* or *sitar,* it can still be done with some difficulty. A *very approximate* idea can be got by playing the harmonium or the piano, taking each note of the scale as the key.

The last sentence above will immediately give the Western reader the clue: the *moorcchana* is nothing more than scalic transposition, which was common with ancient Greek music.

Based on each *moorcchana* a number of melodic types were created which were called *jatis.* It is perhaps from these *jatis* that the current Indian *ragas* bloomed.

By about the 15th cent. A.D. enormous changes in practice and concepts give a new orientation to our music. The idea of *gramas, moorcchanas* and *jatis* disappear, and what remains is a single standard scale (different in North and South), its derivatives resulting in the seventy-two *melas.* A metamorphosis of a very fundamental nature has, therefore, made this ancient music almost unimaginable. It is only from the 17th century onwards that newer concepts and standardization are set in relation to music actually practised.

A melodic system, perhaps distinct from the Aryan, was developed in Southern India. We get information on this music from epics and other works in Tamil of *Sangam* period (2nd to 6th cent. A.D.). The most well-known of these was *Silappadikaram* written by Ilango Adigal. From this and other literature it is surmised that the standard scale of the ancient music of this part of the country was *Sa Ri Ga Ma Pa Dha ni* (C D E F G A B*b*) corresponding to the present *Harikambhoji mela* or *Khamaj thata.* The seven notes were named as *kural, tuttam, kaikkilai, ulai, ili, valari* and *taram;* the microtones were known as *alagus.* The melodic schemata were *panns,* analogous to *ragas,* and *tevarams* or hymns were sung in these.

This whole music slowly came under the influence of Northern styles and systems. A fine rock-cut inscription of the 7th cent. A.D. at Kudimiyamalai in South India is one significant evidence to this incursion. On the rock are inscribed seven *grama ragas* and the note signatures show that they were indicative of names like *shadja, rishabha, gandhara,* etc., all alien to the music of the locale.

Both *jati* and *pann* give place to, rather get modified into, *ragas* of later times. But essentially all of them are the same in the sense that they are all melodic forms. The concept of *raga* is a growth out of the earlier moulds and it has pervaded the entire subcontinent.

The idea of *raga* is at least fifteen centuries old, but even the rules governing the structure of a *raga* have changed with history. Moreover, a single *raga* itself has often undergone modifications in its grammar. What is more, the nomenclature often varies with regions: *Bhairavi* is not the same in the two systems, and *Malkaus* (Hindustani) is known as *Hindolam* in Carnatic music. Again, many melodies which once were popular have gone out of vogue and a number of folk tunes became sophisticated. A common example is the snake-charmer's tune being taken over by concert musicians and made into *raga Punnagavarali.* Great composers of the past like Tyagaraja created new patterns and Tansen is believed to have been responsible for the creation of *ragas* like *Miyanki Todi, Miyanki Malhar* and so on. Even today such changes are taking place.

Conditioned thus by the social and cultural interactions, this kind of musical growth is but natural. *Pari passu* with this have been changes in the system of classification of these melodic types. We have already come across the *jatis* and their grouping under various *moorcchanas.* Later, a very interesting method became popular in North India. This was the *raga-ragini* tradition. Six major melodic genera were postulated and these were called as *ragas* (masculine). They were considered to be of prime importance and deemed as heads of six families. Each *raga* had wives, the *raginis* (feminine) who begot minor *ragas,* the sons. There were also the daughters-in-law of the family. Though the naming of such pedigree appears fanciful to us now, it seems to have had some musical significance.

A beautiful extension of this idea resulted in the personification of *ragas* and *raginis*. Indian aesthetics has a well formulated theory of emotions (the *rasa* theory) wherein different kinds of heroes *(nayaka)* and heroines *(nayika)* have been classified. The details of their states of mind in union and separation have been described to the minutest detail. Originally related to drama and literature, this aesthetic tradition was taken over to music by imagining each *raga* or *ragini* to be a hero or heroine of a particular emotional character. A *raga* becomes a man with a definite feeling in a definite situation; similarly a *ragini* is woman in a dramatic context of her own. For instance, *Malkaus* "wears a robe of blue; he holds a staff in his hand. He wears on his shoulders a string of pearls; he is accompanied by a number of lady attendants. Dressed in blue robe, his shining complexion puts to shame the prince of Kaushaka. With garlands on his shoulders and a white staff in hand, he is the very picture of the purity of the flavour of love. He overpowers the hearts of women and by his beauty attracts the gaze of all. At early dawn he is up and seated. Hero and lover, he is contemplating on his colourful exploits of love." His *ragini, Todi,* beloved of *Malkaus,* "has a complexion of yellow; with saffron and camphor on her body, and is dressed in white robe. Her developed breasts are firm, her waist is thin. Her naval is deep, she has the shine of gold. Her tresses are strings of clouds, her face is the full-moon, in which dance her eyes like those of a fawn and in which shine her teeth like a row of pearls. She wears bejeweled ornaments of incomparable beauty. Venus says to Cupid—'Be sure, do not forget me, if you please'. Her patterned beauty lights up the four quarters; she plays on a *veena*, reposing in a meadow. The strings of the *veena* shine like the rays of effulgence, discoursing melodious music with the sweet *panchama.* She practises the form of the melody in her improvization; by hearing the melody, birds and animals are moved to tears. Absorbed in the songs the fawns dance before her without fear".

This ornate imagery caught the fancy of painters also. Inspired by the human qualities of *ragas* and *raginis,* excellent pictures in colour were created, visualizing the moods and feelings. Known as the *raga-mala* miniatures they are not only interesting as musically evoked paintings but also as some of the finest examples of Indian art *per se.*

The next stage, which was the seed of current methods of classification, begins to take shape about the 15th cent. A.D. Vidyaranya was one of the more important authors who gave a scheme of placing a *raga* under defined scale or *mela*. While this might have been musically satisfactory at the time he lived, the idea was carried to logical conclusion by Venkatamakhi into the schedule of 72 *mela kartas*. It is surmised by some that this change over was due to extraneous—Iranian—influence which brought in the idea of *thata* (the Hindustani word for *mela*). The system, however, has come to stay both in Carnatic and Hindustani music.

The Second Term—Rhythm

TO UNDERSTAND THE nature of rhythm in music one has to see how time is divided (in the first instance), for rhythm is but a particular arrangement of bits of time. Though time is measured by breaking it up mentally, we do use outside adjuncts like clapping hands, beating together of sticks, striking a metal plate or playing on a drum. A very common way of dividing the flow of time familiar to all of us is the ticking of the clock or clapping hands. We shall represent such ticks or claps by ....
.... *ad infinitum.*
All the ticks are uniformly repeated and here we have the simplest breaking up of the stream of time.

If, instead of sounding the ticks in an identical manner, we clap on only every fourth and merely count the intervening ticks without a clap we have—

    (a) 1 2 3 1 2 3 1 2 3 1 2 3 1 2 3
       x . . x . . x . . x . . x . .   *ad infinitum*

where every x is a clap. Again, we may arrange the claps in a slightly different pattern thus:

    (b) 1 21 231212312 12123
       x . x . . x. x.. x . x .x . .   *ad infinitum*

Here, then, are two arrangements, as they divide time in different ways. In (a) there are three counts (one with clap and two without) for every 'section' which may be written as a 3+3 pattern. The design in (b) can be called a 2+3 rhythm.

This series of continuously grouped instants is a simple form of musical rhythm. This is the kind used in Western music. The divisions or sections (or bars, as they are known) are played through in a composition. There is no further ordering of such groupings.

Indian music takes these bars and creates the next order. This process leads to the concept of *tala* which is defined as a recurring arrangement of such patterns.

The essential characteristic of *tala* is its cyclic or repetitive nature. That is, a set of rhythmic units are juxtaposed in a cycle and repeat themselves. This is easy to understand if we compare it to the flow of time and recurrence of week days. Time goes forward in a linear fashion; but superimposed on this stream are the days of the week; a Monday, for example, *repeats* itself making the week a cycle. Similarly musical time flows ahead; superimposed on it is the *tala*, each stroke appearing again and again in the cycle at regular intervals.

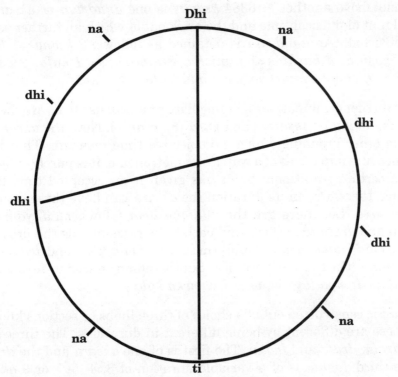

Fig. 4.1 One cycle or *avarta* of ten units *(matras)* divided as 2+3+2+3. This is *Jhaptal* of Hindustani music. Emphatic beat on 1, mild beats on 3 and 8, and a wave of hand on 6. Beat 1 is *sam* and 6 is *khali*.

Let us take a circle of ten beats. Fig. (4.1). Careful scrutiny shows that this really is a 2+3+2+3 rhythm. Again, it is obvious that all the beats are not of the same quality. No. 1 is very emphatic; 3, 8 less so; 6 is vacant. The other beats are similar to one another. If you actually beat the rhythm as follows, a good idea of what this *tala* would sound like can be got.

Give a strong beat on I, faint claps on 3, 8, wave the hand on 6, and count mentally the rest (2, 4, 5, 7, 9, 10), naturally spacing the beats uniformly. What you now counted was one cycle of the *tala* known as *Jhap tal* in North Indian music. One such circle of *tala* is called an *avarta*, meaning 'a cycle' or 'repetition'.

Thus, the whole concept of *tala* has been fitted into a scheme of temporal divisions. This is rigorously followed in Carnatic music; and while it is theoretically recognized in Hindustani music, in practice there are many deviations and exceptions. The basic part of the scheme is the quantification of time, the smallest interval of which is the *ksana* (an instant). This is measured as the time taken "to pierce with a pin one hundred lotus leaves placed one above another". 16384 *ksanas* is one *anudruta* or *aksara*, the practical unit of musical time and the brick out of which all further sections are constructed. (An *anudruta* is obtained as follows: 8 *ksanas*=1 *lava*, 8 *lavas*=1 *kashta*, 8 *kashtas*=1 *nimisha*, 8 *nimishas*= 1 *kala*, 2 *kalas*=1 *chaturbhaga*, and 2 *chaturbhagas*=1 *anudruta*.)

The further combinations of immediate practical use to us are the *druta* (2 *aksaras*), *laghu* (4 *aksaras*) and *guru* (8 *aksaras*). Now, the *aksara* (and hence the other groupings) have no objective time measure. That is, one cannot measure it in terms of a watch or a metronome. It is purely subjective, though a certain traditional habit has given it an accepted time length. Depending, therefore, on its duration the *aksara* can have three degrees of tempo or *laya*. So, there are the *vilamba laya* (slow), *madhyama laya* (medium) and *druta laya* (fast) and each is twice as fast as the preceeding one. Thus *madhyama laya* is double (in speed) of *vilamba*, and *druta* double of *madhyama*. (In the parlance of a South Indian musician *laya* is often called *kala*: *vilamba laya* is, hence, *chowka kala*.)

A *tala* is constructed out of a choice of three limbs or sections known as *anga*. These are different by being different in durations. The three *angas* are *anudruta*, *druta* and *laghu*. The first is of one *aksara* and the *druta* of two. The third, *laghu*, is of a variable duration of 3, 4, 5, 7 or 9 *aksaras*. *Anudruta* is counted by a beat; *druta* by a beat and a wave of the hand; *laghu* by a beat and count of fingers: say, a *laghu* of five units by a beat+counting of four fingers. These three *anudruta*, *druta*, and *laghu* have their own signatures thus:

anudruta: ⌣ druta: o   laghu: |

Since the *laghu* is of five kinds (*jatis*) with varying numbers of *aksaras*, it is shown as : |₃, |₄, |₅, |₇, |₉

The five are given individual names:-

1. l_3=*Tisra laghu* (3 *aksaras*)
2. l_4=*Chaturasra laghu* (4 *aksaras*)
3. l_5=*Khanda laghu* (5 *aksaras*)
4. l_7=*Misra laghu* (7 *aksaras*)
5. l_9=*Sankeerna laghu* (9 *aksaras*)

Now, by the combination of the three *angas* or limbs it is possible to have a variety of *tala-types* :

1.   *Eka tala*— I   (one *laghu*)
2.   *Roopaka tala*—o I   (one *druta*+one *laghu*)
3.   *Matya tala*— lo I   (one *laghu*+one *druta*+one *laghu*)
4.   *Triputa tala*— loo   (one *laghu*+one *druta*+one *druta*)
5.   *Jhampa tala*— lo   (one *laghu*+one *anudruta*+one *druta*)
6.   *Dhruva tala*— lo I I (one *laghu*+one *druta*+one *laghu*+one *laghu*)
7.   *Ata tala*— I loo   (one *laghu*+one *laghu*+one *druta*+one *druta*)

In the above types *(jatis)* the *anudruta* and the *druta* have fixed number of units—one *aksara* and two *aksaras* respectively. Notice that the *laghu* has not been given any definite duration in the list, for it can be of five kinds, as mentioned. So depending on the duration of *laghu,* each *type* can give five different individual *talas.* For instance, *eka tala* is of five varieties:

1. *Tisra jati eka tala* (3 units duration)— l_3
2. *Chaturasra jati eka tala* (4 units duration)— l_4
3. *Khanda jati eka tala* (5 units duration)— l_5
4. *Misra jati eka tala* (7 units duration)— l_7
5. *Sankeerna jati eka tala* (9 units duration)— l_9

As another example, *Jhampa*-type may be studied: Its generic signature is I ˘ o. It can be of the following kinds, each time cycle being a *tala* in its own right.

1. *Tisra jati jhampa tala* l_3˘o=3+1+2=6 *aksaras*
2. *Chaturasra jati jhampa tala* l_4˘o=4+1+2=7 *aksaras*
3. *Khanda jati jhampa tala* l_5˘o=5+1+2=8 *aksaras**
4. *Misra jati jhampa tala* l_7˘o=7+1+2=10 *aksaras*
5. *Sankeerna jati jhampa tala* l_9˘o=9+1+2=12 *aksaras*

Again, *Matya*-type has a generic signature which is | o |.

Five specific *talas* of this genus are:

1. *Tisra jati matya tala* $|_3 o |_3 = 3+2+3 = 8$ *aksaras*
2. *Chaturasra jati matya tala* $|_4 o |_4 = 4+2+4 = 10$ *aksaras*
3. *Khanda jati matya tala* $|_5 o |_5 = 5+2+5 = 12$ *aksaras**
4. *Misra jati matya tala* $|_7 o |_7 = 7+2+7 = 16$ *aksaras*
5. *Sankeerna jati matya tala* $|_9 o |_9 = 9+2+9 = 20$ *aksaras*

In the examples just seen it was the *laghu* that changed, the other two limbs being of constant duration. Thus it is that for every one of the seven types there can be five distinct *talas* and, hence, there are in all 35 *talas* in Carnatic music. This system is said to have been evolved by Purandara-dasa (16th cent), prior to whom there existed a complicated and elaborate system of 108 *talas*. As a matter of fact, the longest cycle in the schedule just described is one of 29 *aksaras*. However, Syama Sastry (18th cent) is credited with a composition in a *tala* of 77 (or was it 256?) *aksaras*, *Sarabha nandana tala*, to defeat the great virtuoso, Bobbili Kesavayya, in a musical contest.

There are two very obvious but important aspects in these arrangements:

First, two or more *talas* may have the total number of *aksaras* and, therefore the duration is the same. But they differ from one another by the distribution of the sections. For example, both *Khanda jati Jhampa tala* and *Tisra jati matya tala* have 8 *aksaras* (each shown by*). But the sections in the former are 5+1+2 and in the latter 3+2+3.

Secondly, there is a strict uniformity about the choice of *laghu*. Once a particular type of this is chosen, the same has to occur throughout the *tala* pattern. For instance, there cannot be a combination like $|_3 o |_4$, as the *laghus* are different. It should either be $|_3 o |_3$ or $|_4 o |_4$. Hindustani music, however, uses such heterogenous combinations as a *Jhumra tal* which is 3+4+3+4.

While there are the 35 *talas* theoretically known and perhaps even learnt, those usually met with in concerts of today are:

1. *Adi tala* (4+2+2)— $|_4 oo$
   (*Chaturasra jati triputa*)

2. *Roopaka tala* (2+4)—o $|_4$
   (*Chaturasra jati rupaka*)

3. *Jhampa tala* (7+1+2)— $|_7 \breve{}o$
   (*Misra jati jhampa*)

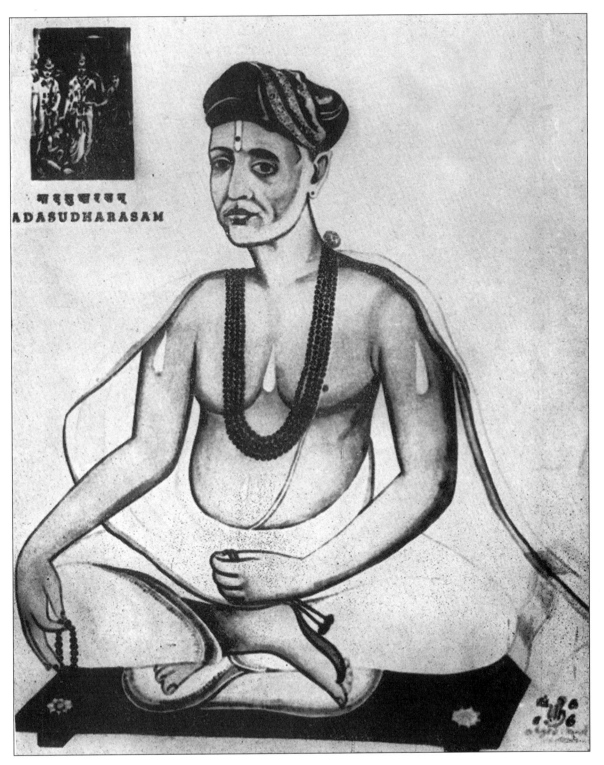

Saint Tyagaraja

Mian Tansen

Mridangam & Tabla class in progress

Nadaswaram

The violin: Indian style of playing

The sarangi

The veena

The sitar

The sarod

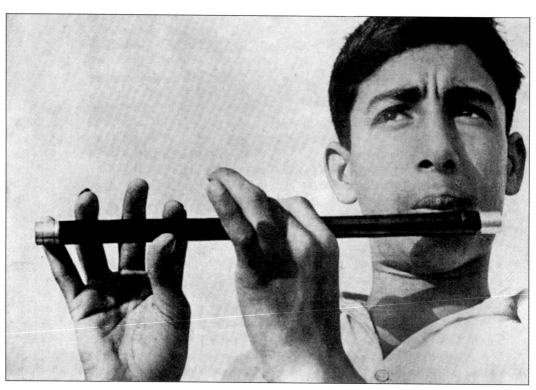

The horizontal flute

The jaltarang

The santoor, Kashmir

The pakhawaj

The tabla

4. *Chapu tala* (3+4)
   (Misra chapu)

5. *Khanda chapu tala* (2+3)

In actual practice *Roopaka* is not set as 2+4, but often as 2+2+2. It will also be of interest to note that the *Chapu tala* does not fall within the scheme of 35 *talas*. Is it borrowed from folk music without much sophistication?

The basic concept and construction of *tala* in Hindustani music is on the same lines as described. In both the systems it is conceived as a cyclic measure; again, both create it by the additions of time units *(aksara* or *matra)* and the sectional divisions. However, there are some differences worth observing.

The fundamental unit of time in North Indian music is *matra* which is equivalent to the *anudruta* or *aksara* of the Southern music. Here again the *matra* is of an arbitrary and subjective time value. It may be long, medium or short in duration. When long it gives a slow *(vilambit),* when medium a *(madhya)* and when short a fast *(drut)* tempo. But there is one difference in actual practice between the two systems of Indian music. In Carnatic music the proportion of the three *layas* is kept—i.e., the *madhyama* is strictly twice in speed of the *vilamba* and the *druta* twice of *madhyama:* as the musicians there say, there is an adherence to *kala pramana* (temporal ratio). But in North India, particularly in current singing of *kheyal* and playing of instruments, there is no such strictness. The tempo is gradually increased from very slow to very fast. A rhythmic composition is usually started in *vilambit laya* and the artiste gradually works it out to increasing tempos; but there is no measured acceleration. Sometimes separate compositions are performed for slow and fast music. However, in the *dhrupad* style of singing a uniformity of tempo is maintained throughout.

The sections of *tala,* what was the *anga,* is commonly called a *khand* in Hindustani music. Of these the common ones are *anudruta* (one *matra*), the *druta* (two *matras*). The use of the idea of *laghu* as in South India is not there. A *laghu* in the North is of four *matras,* the other types not being employed. The larger sections of the *tala* can be of 3, 4, 5 or more *matras.* What is of greater importance, a *tala* can have heterogenous *laghus,* a fact not met with in Carnatic music. For instance, the rhythmic cycles *Deepchandi* and *Jhumra* have *khandas* as 3+4+3+4. That is, there is addition of different kinds of *laghus* (*tisra* and *chaturasra jati*). There are *talas* which use even more complicated arrangements: for instance, *Pasupati tala* has a form 5+7+9+5, and *Dhuruva tala* has 7+3+1+9+6+3. Rare time cycles of even 9-1/4 *matras* have also been described, but such combinations are more arithmetic jugglery than musical practice. Today, following are the commonly heard:

1.	*Kaharuva tal*	:	4	*matras*
2.	*Dadra tal*	:	3+3	*matras*
3.	*Roopak tal*	:	3+2+2	*matras*
4.	*Jhaptal*	:	2+3+2+3	*matras*
5.	*Ektal*	:	4+4+2+2	*matras*
6.	*Chautal*	:	2+2+2+2+2+2	*matras*
7.	*Deepchandi tal*	:	3+4+3+4	*matras*
8.	*Dhamar tal*	:	5+2+3+4	*matras*
9.	*Jhumra tal*	:	3+4+3+4	*matras*
10.	*Tilvada tal*	:	4+4+4+4	*matras*
11.	*Trital*	:	4+4+4+4	*matras*

We may notice a curious fact; both *Trital* and *Tilvada* have sixteen units divided identically. So is the case with *Jhumra* and *Deepchandi*. What then is the difference between such pairs? The contrast lies in the emphasis of the beats as well as the finer internal distributions of time which 'fill' the *matras*. Thus the same number of time units can be arranged into similar bars, but may give different *talas* because of emphasis within the limits of the sections. We shall return to this a little later.

Of all the positions in the cycle or *avarta* there are two which are of great significance: *sam (sama)* and *khali*.

The *sam* is the first beat of the *tala*. It is the most emphatic of all moments and strokes, as it commences the cycle. All compositions are set such that their burdens always fall on this initiating beat. It is a kind of centre of gravity of the whole circle; and the melodic and rhythmic variations that a musician creates invariably come to a close on this and it would be an unpardonable lapse if he misses it out of confusion. The *sam* is so important—musically as well as aesthetically—that listeners will respond, quite vocally, with exclamations of approval, when the singer or player arrives at the *sam* with a fine dexterity after cycles of improvizations: it is what they have been waiting for!

The next in order of rhythmic centricity is *khali*. The word literally means 'vacant', 'empty'. It is shown, usually, by a wave of the hand, without giving an audible beat. (In Carnatic music it is called *veesu* or *visarjitam*.) Normally *khali* indicates the middle of a section or bar. (But in a number of *talas* it assumes greater weight. For, in these it also commences the middle

of the *avarta.*) For example, in *Jhaptal* the sixth is a *khali* (o), while the first
is the *sam* (x):

> *Jhaptal* : 1 2 / 3 4 5 / 6 7 / 8 9 10
>   x   o

In *Trital* the ninth *matra* is *khali:*

> 1 2 3 4 / 5 6 7 8 / 9 10 11 12 / 13 14 15 16
> x   o

The importance of *khali* in such a context is that it is an indicator of the
approaching *sam*. Since the whole tension is built up for reaching the first
beat, the *khali* acts as a signal telling the musician to close his melodic
patterns. The drummer shows the *sam* by a 'hard' stroke and the *khali* by a
'soft' one and the main singer or player often takes this as a cue for keeping
to the *tala.*

This aspect of drumming has become an art of finest beauty and
consummate skill. The drummer and the main artiste have not only to keep
to *laya* and *tala,* but their virtuosity is tested by the cross rhythmic and
complementary patterns they combine. The strokes or rhythmic syllables,
therefore, have been developed to as great a finesse as melodic differentia in
ragas. Each stroke has been given a name: if a *table* is beaten on the rim
with the forefinger it is *na* or *ta,* the left drum beaten flat gives *kat* and so
on. The right face of the *mridanga* struck at the centre with the fingers
produces *nam, tam.* Such mnemonics are known as *bol, jati, solkattu* and by
other names in various regions and they are the finger ingredients that go
to make the rhythmic figures. The strokes and pauses are arranged to create
innumerable patterns of breathtaking complexity. Improvization of such a
nature is indeed very difficult, but, when created by a master musician, is a
thing of extraordinary beauty. Normally, however, the permutations and
combinations of *bols* are pre-set and the rhythmic designs produced from
these are of many varieties and are distinguished by various names.

Of particular interest is the definition of a *tala* by these mnemonics.
This is specially so in North India. Every *tala* has been assigned a basic set
of *bols* and the set is called a *theka;* and a *tala* is identified by its *theka.* For
instance, the *theka* of *Jhaptal* is:

> *dhi na / dhi dhi na / ti na / dhi dhi na*
>
> 1   3   6   8
>
> x   o

The *theka for Trital* is:

dha dhin dhin dha / dha dhin dhin dha /
1   5
x

dha tin tin na / ta dhin dhin dha
9   13
o

When a composition in a *tala* is sung or played, the drummer will give only this set of *bols,* in the beginning. That is, he will commence with the *theka* of the *tala.* All other combinations will come later. The two concepts— *tala* and *theka*—have become so fused that students are taught the *theka* right in the beginning of the *tala* lessons. Notice in the above examples that the *sam* (x) gets a hard consonant and the *khali* (o) or its section soft ones.

The *theka* is so significant and important that *talas* with the same number of units *(matras)* and similar sections get differentiated by their *thekas;* for a distinguishable rhythmic emphasis is thus obtained. For example, there are two *talas, Trital* and *Tilvada,* which have sixteen units each, grouped as 4+4+4+4; but they are treated as separate because the *internal* distribution of *bols* in the *thekas* are not the same, giving rise to different feelings of time. The *theka* of *Trital* has already been given. The basic pattern of *Tilvada* is played thus:

dha tirakita dhi tadhi / na na ti ti
1   5
x
ta tirakita dhi tadhi / na na dhi dhi
9   13
o

The differences are obvious and the dynamic feeling is easily experienced. Another pair of *talas* illustrates the point: *Jhumra* and *Deepchandi.* Both have fourteen units arranged as 3+4+3+4. But their *internal* emphasis differs:

Jhumra :   dhi-dha tirakita /
             1
             o

dhi dhi dhage tirakita/

4

ti-ta tirakita/

8

o

dhi dhi dhage tirakita

II

Deepchandi:

dha dhin—/

1

o

dha dha dhin—/

4

ta tin—/

8

o

dha dha dhin

II

The—(dash) represents a period of silence when there is no stroke at all. Notice the different placement of these silences. Such emphasis by negativity gives each of these *talas* a characteristic flavour of its own.

Rhythm, like melody, has been raised to a high degree of sophistication. Besides the division and distribution of time in *tala* and the art of drumming, the compositions and their relation to *tala*, the cross rhythms and syncopations; in actual performance are further facets of this fascinating but difficult art. So it was said that the first necessity in music was the control of rhythm, for otherwise "the song (and dance) will go out of control, like a wild elephant without the check of *ankusa* (the elephant driver's hook) and the knowledge of Time is unlimited and even Siva has not the capacity to cross over its Limitlessness."

5

Form and Style

INDIAN MUSIC HAS recognized two broad categories of musical forms: the open and the closed, roughly equivalent to and reminiscent of the ancient *anibaddha* and *nibaddha*. The word *anibaddha* means 'not bound'. That is, the music is not set without the limitations of a framework like a song. It has no rhythmic structure or defined sectional arrangements. The *nibaddha,* on the other hand means 'bound' or 'set within a frame'. A song or an instrumental piece with definite parts, set to a *tala* and having a defined beginning and end is a *nibaddha* form. Another word generally used for a closed form, particularly a song, is *prabandha*—that which is well bound; the current English translation of this is 'composition'.

The most important *anibaddha sangeeta* is the *alap*. Here the *raga* is developed and elaborated slowly, note by note, phrase by phrase. Due prominence is given to the emphatic notes (*vadi, samvadi,* etc.), characteristic phrases *(anga)* and graces. The usual practice is to start with the lower pitches and very gradually work up. A certain set of notes is taken as the base and variations of this theme are improvised unfolding the form of the *raga*. As a matter of fact, the *alap* is the most sensitive and fundamental part of *raga* enunciation. The most delicate aspects of melodic progressions are possible only in *alap* and good musicians have always felt—perhaps, rightly—that it is mainly in this section that a *raga* exhibits its correct form. Vowels like *a,ee,o* and so on are used while singing it. 'Words' such as *tere, dere, re, na, nom, tom* are also employed and these are supposed to be derived from *'Om anantam' (Om* Infinite) and *'Om Hari Anantam'* and, *'Om Hari Narayana'*. In South Indian music, in singing *dhrupad* (North India) and in all instrumental music, *alap* always proceeds the rhythmic compositions. However, in the *kheyals* of Hindustani music (except in a 'school' called the Agra *gharana*) it is incorporated into the composition itself during elaboration. This may be done with plain vowels and/or with the words of the songs. In the latter case it is called *bol alap*—that is, an *alap* executed with the help of *bols* (words). There is no rhythmic accompaniment to the *alap*—at least it is never bound by *tala*. But a sense of proportion of duration of notes governs its structure. However, when it is part of an elaboration of a *kheyal,* there is a coordination between the closure of melodic patterns and the *tala*.

In Hindustani music, an instrumentalist will follow up the *alap* with a faster movement called *jod*. Musical phrases follow one another in fairly quick succession and are more intricate. Here again there is no *tala*. The *jod* is succeeded by *jhala* which again is devoid of *tala*. Here, both the main strings of the instrument and the drone strings *(chikari)* are used. They are played alternately, varying in strokes and patterns, generally in a fast tempo. Though unattached to *tala, jod* and *jhala* have an obvious rhythmic character which easily distinguishes them from *alap*.

Fast phrases are called *tans* in Hindustani music. The patterns are complicated, note coming after note, weaving patterns at moderate and quick tempos. There are any number of varieties of such quick movements, as for instance: a *tan* may be a straight ascent or descent when it is called a *saral* or *sapat tan;* if it is tortuous, it is *vakra* or *kuta tan*. When sung with the words of the song, it is a *bol-tan*. (Instrumentalists use a corresponding word *'palta'*). The *tans* are rarely, if ever, sung independently of a composition; they generally form the climax of musical rendering, closing the unfoldment of the presentation of a *raga*. Some musicians use the word *tan* in a different context, for by *tan* they also mean the characteristic phrase of a *raga:* what was called *chalan, pakad* and so on earlier in the chapter on *raga*.

In Carnatic music an *alapana* is followed by a *tanam* (not to be confounded with *tan*). The singer employs syllables like *tanam, nam, tam* and so on. These are mutilations of the words *'Om Anantam',* meaning *'Om Infinite'*. It is also played on instruments in imitation of the voice. While free of *tala*, it is faster than the *alapa* and resembles, in a way, the *jod* of Hindustani instrumental music.

A way of presentation, common to South India and North India, but particularly to the former, is singing the melodic line using the signatures of notes: sol-fa singing. It is known as *kalpana svara* in the South and *sargam* in the North. (The word *sargam* is a combination of the first four note-signatures—*Sa, Ri, Ga, Ma*). Instead of singing the *raga* with a plain vowel or with the words of the song, the note-signatures are used *(Sa, Ri, Ga, Ma, Pa, Dha, Ni)*.

Neraval is a typical open form of Carnatic system. In Hindustani music we have already met the *bol-tan*, a fast phrase sung with the libretto *(bol)*.

A very similar musical idiom found in the South is the *'neraval'*. Certain sections of the song are chosen and the words of these phrases are sung with more and more complex melodic and rhythmic emphasis and variations.

All these are *anibaddha* in the sense that they are 'open' structures: that is, they have no strictly determined beginning or end; neither do they have sections following one another in a preconceived design with formal *tala*. In other words, they are not 'compositions' or songs. They are, however, introduced into a composition while improvising and as such have no independent existence outside it, except, of course, *alapa, jod, jhala* and *tanam*.

It is very necessary to understand the musical situation of what has been called the 'open' form. They are contra distinct to the 'closed' but not necessarily independent of the latter. For instance, *alap, jod,* and *tanam* are not bound by a song. They are executed before the composition is begun. But *bol-tans* and *neraval* are of necessity elaborations and improvization of a phrase in the song. But they are not composed as a song is: their structures are not predetermined. They are introduced into the unfoldment of the melody of a song or a composition and form variations of the textual or compositional melodic theme.

Closed Forms

Nibaddha sangeeta is one in which there are meaningful words or set tunes to a definite rhythm. More simply put, it is a song or an instrumental piece, with predetermined beginning and end.

A 'composition' here should not be taken as equivalent to a composition in Western music. A song or an instrumental piece in Indian music is a kind of peg to hang the *raga* elaboration on. In a performance, the *alap* and the variations of the *raga* theme are the major aspects. The composition is there to guide the musician in setting a rhythmic pace and a melodic design. Every composition is a basic mould for such variations which are improvised on the spot.

Current Closed Forms in Hindustani Music

Dhruvapada : 15th and 16th centuries A.D. saw in North India the acme of a style and composition called the *dhruvapada* or *dhrupad* which seems to have developed from more ancient compositional types, *dhruva prabandhas*. This was the time of a general revival of and exuberance in various walks of life, patronized by benign and enlightened rulers like Raja Mansingh Tomar of Gwalior and Emperor Akbar. It was the age that produced great *dhrupad* singers like Swami Haridas, Tansen, Baiju Bavra and others. The form is existent to this day, though not very popular or widespread.

In structure, *dhrupad* has four sections. Of these the *asthayi* or *sthayi* is the basic and first part. It opens the composition and is usually in the lower and middle octaves. The *antara* is the second section and moves in the middle and upper octaves. The complexities of *raga* and compositional intricacies are further developed in the succeeding two sections—*sanchari* and *abhog*. However, as heard at present, only the first two parts are common. The *talas* generally used are *Chautal* (4+4+2+2), *Teevra* (3+2+2) and *Jhaptal* (2+3+2+3). When the *prabandha* (song) is in *Jhaptal* it is often called a *sadra*.

Dhrupad singing always starts with an *alap,* in slow, medium and fast tempos. The *prabandha* is sung next, with main emphasis on rhythmic designs and syncopations. The entire atmosphere is one of grandeur and gravity. There is a certain kind of softness in some styles, but rarely if ever, is there an attempt to make it a filigree. *Dhamar* is another variety of this type, generally similar to *dhrupad.* However, it is less grave in melodic progressions. The literary content of *dhamar* describes the play of Lord Krishna, particularly in the Festival of Colours *(Holi).* The *tala* is always *Dhamar* of fourteen *matras.*

There were four styles or *vanis* of singing *dhrupad.* The *Gauhar vani,* of which the best known musician was Tansen, emphasized melodic glides in severe straight lines. The *Dagar vani,* on the other hand, tended to develop the melody on curved lines and subtle graces. The *Khandara vani* seems to have been known for its quick embellishments with full-throated singing and the *Nauhar vani* for its broad jumps. There is a couplet that says, "Loudly sung is the *Khandar vani,* sweet speaks the *Nauhar; Gauhar* requires much breath and the *Dagar* is predominantly of *alap*". *Vani* literally means speech or a style of utterance. Even today this word, modified as *bani,* is used in South India to mean style. These *vanis* of *dhrupad* are no more found in very distinct forms now and even *dhrupad* as a genre is not widely sung at present.

Kheyal : The most common and currently accepted as the highest stage of musical art in North India is the *kheyal.* The word *kheyal* is itself not Indian but Persian, and means an 'idea' or 'imagination'. In comparison to *dhrupad,* which is sombre, *kheyal* is more free and flowery. However, it lacks the epic quality of the former.

How exactly *kheyal* originated is not yet clear. It is conjectured that it was a further sophistication of what was known as *rupaka alapti* in ancient India. But it is also quite possible that migrant Central and Mid-Asian musicians developed and modified some indigenous music into *kheyal.* For, it is said that Amir Khusro (13th cent.) and later Sultan Mohammad Sharqui (15th cent.) gave it a fillip and wider currency. The credit of making it an art of high order is given to Niyamat Khan '*Sadarang*' and his nephew (?) '*Adarang*' (18th cent.). Today *kheyal* is the most respected class of music and no usual concert of vocal music will commence without it and some of the finest singers for the past one century belonged to this group.

A *kheyal* has two parts: *sthayi* (or *asthayi*) and *antara*. The former has its movements generally in the lower and middle octaves, and all melodic variations and improvisations end with the last few phrases of this section; it is for this reason that this initial part is called *sthayi*, for the word means 'stable'. In essence it is the burden of the song and performance. The second part, *antara*, is sung after the *sthayi*. Its progressions are in the middle and upper octaves. The two sections are complementary to each other and together they give a full picture of the *raga* framework in all the registers, as they guide the musician in further elaborations. The manner in which a *kheyal* is composed determines the style of extemporization and a good musician will always bear in mind the melodic and rhythmic design of the song *(cheez)* and evolve the music to suit this mood.

There are two kinds of *kheyals: bada kheyal* and *chota* (the big and the small). Both are similar to the extent of having two sections, *sthayi* and *antara*. The *bada kheyal* is composed to suit slower tempos with a structure that can accommodate *alap* and movements in medium tempo. The mood, though not as ponderous as *dhrupad*, is still grave and the best exposition of a *raga* can be done mainly in this *kheyal*. The singing of a *bada kheyal* is followed by a *chota kheyal* in the same *raga*, though not necessarily in the same *tala*. This is in medium and fast tempos. No detailed *alap* is introduced; *tans, bol tans, sargam* and cross rhythmic patterns predominate.

The *bada kheyal* is commenced with the *sthayi* in slow or medium tempo. After the text is sung for one or two cycles of *tala*, the *alap* either with a plain vowel or with the words of the song *(bol-alap)* is introduced, the *tala* cycles continuing. The musician will elaborate and improvise, and his merit is in making an artistic return to *sam* (first beat of the cycle of rhythm) after every improvization. As the *raga* blossoms out, the melody begins to cover greater ranges. Then the *antara* is sung. Now the patterns become quicker and more intricate. At the proper time, the *chota kheyal* is begun, when the music becomes faster and a climax with very quick *tans, sargams* (sol-fa), *bol tans* (melodic textual variations) completes the recital. All the while the nucleus of attention is the *sam* to which the melody must return again and again.

As in *dhrupad,* there are four major schools of *kheyal.* They are popularly known as *gharanas* which literally means 'houses' or 'families'. They, as well as, the *vanis* of *dhrupad* may be compared to the dialects of a language. The differences lie in the manner of enunciation, musical idioms and accents, but the structure of a *raga* is the same in all these 'schools'. The oldest and the most comprehensive in technique is the *Gwalior gharana.* The doyens of this school were Natthan Khan and Peer Baksh, who settled in Gwalior. Hassu Khan and Haddu Khan (19th cent.), sons of Natthan Khan, evolved a style which has since then come to be called the *Gwalior gharana.* The qualifying characteristics are open-throated singing and straight movements. The *bada kheyal* is usually sung in a medium tempo, with the *sthayi* sung twice fully and then the *antara.* It is only then that *alap,* etc. are elaborated. Due emphasis is given to rhythmic play. The *Agra gharana* is said to have been 'founded' by Haji Sujan Khan, the son-in-law(?) of Tansen. Sujan Khan himself was no *kheyal* singer but a *dhrupadiya.* But a descendent of his, *Gagghe* Khuda Baksh (18th-19th cent.), took to *kheyal* out of sheer disappointment, they say, at his inability to perform *dhrupad.* He went to Natthan Khan at Gwalior and learnt *kheyal* and later returned to Agra and around him grew this *gharana.* So Sujan Khan being the 'founder' is more a family ancestry than a musical lineage. Open-throated singing, with emphasis on *bol tan* and rhythmic syncopation are its peculiarities. Also, it is close to the *dhrupadic* form and, like it, the *alap* is sung before the *kheyal,* using syllables such as *nom, tom.* The songs are in medium tempo. One of the greatest vocalists of recent times, Faiyyaz Khan, (20th cent.) was of this school; but he gave it a new and pleasant lyrical colour so that his style was better known as the *Rangeela gharana* (lyrical school).

A third major school is the *Jaipur-Atroli gharana.* It is associated with the great singer Alladiya Khan (19th-20th cent.). The style is characterised by medium tempo with *tans* growing out of repetitive patterns or *alankaras.* The more recent Patiala school, however, specializes in quick and complicated phrases. The fourth major school, also modern, is now becoming popular. It was developed mainly by Abdul Wahid Khan and Abdul Karim Khan of the last generation, and is known as the *Kirana gharana.* Very pleasant to hear, there is an insistence on slow tempo in the *bada kheyal* with gradual growth of *alap.* It is fine filigree work and rarely uses broad jumps and tortuous movements.

Besides *dhrupad* and *kheyal,* North India has two very important musical forms: *thumri* and *tappa. Thumri* is very lyrical in approach. Here the words, generally, romantic in import, have as much a dominant role as the music, unlike *dhrupad* and *kheyal* where music is of first importance. Again, not all *ragas* are used for *thumri;* and those that are used are amenable to this mood of soft and fine sentiments—e.g. *Khamaj, Kafi, Bhairavi, Pilu* and so on. The grammar is also much laxer and a musician often mixes *ragas.* The whole aim here is to create an atmosphere of romance and what the Indian calls as *sringara:* a love song describing the joy of union, the pangs of separation, uncertainty of anticipation and nostalgia of memory. There are, broadly, two styles of *thumri.* One is the *Poorab* (Eastern) variety, where the manner of exposition is slow and rather subdued. The Punjab style on the other hand is more mercurial.

It is said that the songs of camel drivers of North-West have become refined into the classical *tappa.* Usually composed in Punjabi language, *tappa* is recognized by very quick turns of phrase with no slower elaboration. This form has not spread very wide even in upper India; though generally confined to North and North-West, a fine class of *tappas* was composed in Bengal about a century ago. *Tappa* singers of good quality are not easily met with now and it is slowly getting extinct.

Tarana is a commonly heard type. Here no meaningful words are used. Instead, 'nonsense' syllables like *dere, tere, nadir, yalali* and so on are woven into a rhythmic piece in a *raga.* Some say that these are adaptations of mnemonic signatures of the *tabla* and *sitar* strokes; some others, on the other hand, are of the opinion that these syllables are mutilations of Persian and Arabic words. A *tarana* is generally, though not always, composed in a fast tempo. No slow phrases are interpolated; but the melodic improvization is done using these 'nonsense' sounds in *tans.*

The forms so far described are of dual characters. It is very important to understand this: that these categories (except the *tarana*) are both compositions and manners of presentation. For example, *kheyal* is a composition with two sections; this song is itself called a *cheez, bandish* or *kheyal.* But any song with two parts is not a *kheyal.* For *kheyal* is also a particular approach and manner of rendition which depends on the voice production, kinds of grace, sequence of exposition and so on.

Closed Forms in Carnatic Music

The *varnam* is one of the basic types of compositions. It is generally, though not necessarily, considered an excellent exercise for teaching and practice; but a concert is often begun with a good *varnam.* It is composed in such a way that it shows the characteristic phrases, states, melodic movements of a *raga,* and an insight into the structure of *varnam* leads to insight into the structure of the *raga.* A *varnam* has two parts: the *poorvanga* which again has three sections—*pallavi, anupallavi* and *muktayi svara. Pallavi* is the opening and the burden of the song; the second and complementary part is the *anupallavi* and the concluding one is the *muktayi svara.* The second part comprises the *uttaranga* or *ettukadai,* having sections *(charana)* which are arranged in successively increasing complexity. Two kinds of *varnam* are known: the *pada varnam* (or *chowka varnam*) which is made up *entirely* of meaningful text *(sahitya) and* the *tana varnam* wherein the composition is partly of text and partly of solfeggio *(svara* names) passages.

The most popular and considered the finest form is the *kriti,* sometimes also called *keertana.* Its great popularity and wide acceptance is due to the inherent viability in melodic growth and rhythmic elasticity, as the text and music permit great freedom for creative improvization. *Kriti* means 'a creation, that which is made'. *Keertana* is 'to sing'. The word generally used now is *kriti* and it is in this form that we come across the finest compositions. In a *keertana,* which more particularly refers to a devotional song, it is the poetic beauty of the song that predominates: in the *kriti,* on the other hand, music is more important. The Tallapakam composers (14th-15th cent.) are credited with the earliest *kritis.* They wrote mostly in Telugu and arranged their *kritis* into *pallavi, anupallavi* and *charana.* Though the music of these songs is lost, their texts are even today available inscribed on copper plates.

A *kriti* has three sections: *pallavi, anupallavi* and *charana,* which we had already met in the *varnam.* The word *pallavi* is perhaps derived from '*pallava*'—to blossom, for this section opens the composition. Like the *sthayi* in *kheyal* it is the commencing part and the burden. It is also generally restricted to lower and middle octaves. *Anupallavi* means "that which follows the *pallavi*". Its movements are usually in the middle and upper registers, comparable to the *antara.* Thus the *pallavi* and *anupallavi* are complementary to each other; between the two they reveal the full features of the *raga.* There may be one or more *charanas* following the *anupallavi* (*charana* means foot); and *charana* combines the qualities of both *pallavi* and *anupallavi.* A good *kriti* is so knit, both in text and music, that *anupallavi* and *charana* end and dovetail into the *pallavi* which is repeated after them as the main theme of the song. The singing of *kriti,* apart from its sectional order, is characterized and beautified by other decorative phrases. Of these *sangati, chitta svara, neraval* and *kalpana svara* (solfeggio) are commonly met with.

Sangati is a kind of built-in variation of a phrase of the *kriti.* After the main phrase is sung in the originally composed basic melodic line, it is repeated again and again with slight changes every time. These variations of phrase are *sangatis* and are often made by the composer himself. However, an eminent musician introduces a *sangati* which, finding an acceptance, is handed over traditionally. Every performer will sing or play all the traditional *sangatis* in the known order following one another with greater intricacy and length, before introducing his own musical themes.

Chitta svara is another pre-conceived part of a *kriti*. It is a solfeggio or *svara* singing, composed and ready-made. The composer of the song or a distinguished artiste constructs a *chitta svara,* which is a set of *svara* in the *raga* and *tala* of the *kriti,* and incorporated in the song; and this is sung or played with the composition without alteration. Of course, not every *kriti* has a *chitta svara.*

While *chitta svara* forms the predetermined and, therefore, unalterable part of a *kriti* the improvisational additions are usually two: *neraval* and *kalpana svara.* We have already come across these as *anibaddha* forms. Their essential quality, in contrast to *chitta svara,* is that they are the musician's on-the-spot creations, not pre-designed music. Both in *neraval* and *kalpana svara,* as in *bol tan,* there is always a very fine syncopation and crossing of rhythmic patterns of the *tala.*

What *thumri* and *tappa* are to Hindustani music, *padam* and *javali* are to Carnatic music, though in construction they are entirely different. *Padam* and *javali* have one aspect in common—their texts and music are more lyrical than *kritis* and are generally love songs. Both are, therefore, used for dances. Again, both have *pallavi, anupallavi* and *charana. Padams,* however, are slower in tempo and graver in import. Further, it is usual to treat them as allegoric: that is, the love-life sung in human terms really refer to the yearning of the human mind for the Adored Godhead. This, of course is a common and fundamental feature of all the music inspired by the *bhakti* movement (a socio-religious upsurge of devotion). The greatest of such songs are the Sanskrit *astapadis* of Jayadeva (12th cent.) and the Telugu *padams* of Kshetrayya (17th cent.). The physiological and psychological love between man and woman are sublimated and 'elevated' to high mystic Adoration *(madhura bhakti).* The separation, the union, the misunder-standings between the hero *(nayaka)* and the heroine *(nayika)* are delicately described with superb sensitivity and this beauty is expressed through dance and the attuned music of *padams. Javalis* are also love lyrics sung to suitable *ragas.* But they are not generally considered as allegoric. They are direct descriptions of human love, portrayed with fine understanding in text, music (which is faster in tempo than in a *padam)* and dance.

Tillana is the Carnatic counterpart of the *tarana* of North India. While it has *pallavi, anupallavi* and *charana,* the libretto is usually of *jatis (tala* mnemonics) combined with *svara* signatures and sometimes a few meaningful words. *Tillana* is not generally of slow tempo. Besides being sung in the later part of a concert, it invariably is an item in the repertoire of a dancer.

Musically most complicated and developed is the *pallavi*. We have already come across this word as the opening part of a *kriti*. But *pallavi* here is very much different. It is not a part of *kriti,* but a style of presentation of a *raga*. In spirit and technique it roughly corresponds to the *bada kheyal* of Hindustani music. Speaking in very general terms *pallavi* can be thought of as a further elaboration of *neraval* and the word *pallavi* is usually considered as a derived from three others: *pada* (word), *laya* (tempo) and *vinyasa* (elaboration), the first syllables of the three words forming 'pallavi'. In rendering it a musician will start with an *alap,* unravelling the *raga* in great detail. This is followed by a *tanam*. Then a set line of a song (the *pallavi* proper) is begun. This may be specially composed or taken from a known piece. It is a common practice to have the *pallavi* of one *tala* cycle, though longer compositions are known. There is no *anupallavi* or *charana*. The tempo is slow and the melodic piece chosen is more a base for bringing out the niceties of the *raga* and the *tala*. The unfoldment develops from slow and simpler phrases to faster and complicated improvizations. Beautiful and intricate patterns, both in *raga* and *tala,* are woven with much care and expertise, with *neraval, kalpana svara* and rhythmic variations, and it is a test of talent and imagination of both the principal musician and the accompanists. After a very elaborate performance of the main *raga,* the *pallavi* is sometimes concluded with a *raga-malika* (a garland of *ragas*). That is, keeping the tempo and the *tala* the same, the test is sung/played in a variety of *ragas*. The choice of such *ragas* which succeed one another rapidly has no rigid rule. The musician varies the *raga* according to his mood and capacity. Sometimes he may introduce the *raga-malika* not in the *pallavi* proper but in the *tanam*. *Pallavi* rendering is generally concluded by a *tani avartam*. This part is meant for the percussionists: the players of *mridangam, ghatam* and *kanjira*. Exciting syncopations and cross rhythms are played, one vying with another; and they all have to observe and match the *tala* figures created by the main musician. The *pallavi*, thus, is a very elaborate and dignified rendering of a *raga,* and *tala,* and the demand on the musicians is not small. That is why the real test of maturity and virtuosity of an artiste lies in his *pallavi*.

Besides the compositional types of classical music described so far, India has an enormous variety of devotional songs. Indeed, most of the classical compositions have as their literary content devotional themes. Particularly after the *bhakti* movement, these have formed a link between the classical and folk music; for their tunes are generally in some *raga* or the other and their words convey deep piety. Yet they have a simplicity that appeals to both the musically initiated and the lay.

In North India the major forms are *bhajan, keertan* of Bengal and *abhanga* of Maharashtra. *Bhajans* are sung throughout the North. The subject is the praise of the Lord: descriptions of the lives and deeds of Rama, Krishna or Siva and beseeching Him for grace. Some of the finest *bhajans* have been written by great mystics like Kabir, Nanak, Surdas and Meera. Their purport and music are simple and hence the musically untrained also can sing them. It may be a lone ministerial or a *samaj* (congregation), but there can be few who are unmoved by this delicate music. Similarly *keertan* of Bengal is a traditional institution and not merely a way of singing. Drawing inspiration from the immortal *Gita Govinda* of Jayadeva, it was transformed into a song and dance congregation by that mystic of mystics, Sri Chaitanya (15th-16th cent). In Maharashtra *abhangas* of saints Eknath (16th cent.), Jnaneswar (13th cent.), Tukaram (16th-17th cent.), and the *bhajans* of Narsi Mehta in Gujarat and a host of others have seeped deep and wide into the hearts of the people.

In the South, some of the earliest known hymns were the *tevaram*. Composed by the three saints, Tirujnana Sambandar, Tirunavukkarasu (Appar) and Sundaramurthy Nayanar (7th-9th cent., A.D.), they formed the foundations of the musical culture of the Tamil speaking people. *Tevarams* were sung in various *panns* (analogous to *ragas*) by a class of singers known as the *oduvars* and others. There are also the *Tiruvachakam* of Manikkavachakar, the *Tiruppugazh* of Arunagirinathar. In Telugu the songs of Tallapakam brothers (15th cent.) were the foremost of not only devotional *keertanas* but also the earliest known compositions with sectional arrangement of *pallavi, anupallavi* and *charana*. Bhadrachala Ramadas (17th cent.), who was praised in great humility by even Tyagaraja, was a great devotee and sang many a *keertana*. These are some of the finest songs in Telugu, at once homely in diction and transparent in piety. The *utsava sampradaya keertana* and *divya nama keertana* of Tyagaraja to this day form a part of prayer in any devotional singing. It is in Kannada that we come across songs of Adoration—*devara nama* (God's name)—of extraordinary number. In 16th century there appeared the saint-singer, Sri Purandaradasa, who went round the land with his *tambura* and *chipla* (hand clappers) as a mendicant, preaching the beauty of adoration. He is said to have composed 4,75,000 songs. Others in this lineage were Kanakadasa and Jagannathadasa, to mention only two.

It is in such songs of piety and wisdom that some of the most beautiful music of India lives. They are not only musically attractive, devoid of the dryness of the intellectual virtuoso, but preach a simplicity of living. A Chaitanya, a Tukaram or a Purandara can bring greater peace and love to a naive villager than any learned preacher.

Compositions for Instruments

While the closed forms so far discussed are for the voice, compositions for instruments are different in Hindustani music. Such pieces are called *gats*. *Gats* which are set to definite *ragas* and *talas* have *sthayi* and *antara* as in a *kheyal*. The musical structure, as far as *raga* and *tala* rules are concerned, is also the same. The difference lies in exploiting the possibilities of the instrument. In a plucked instrument, for instance, all the advantages of plucked strokes, deflection of strings, finger pressure, glides and so on are the elements which go to make the characteristics of instrumental *gat* and technique. Naturally, the tonal qualities and range of the instrument will have much to say in this. Compositions for bowed instruments will be slightly of a different make-up. However, even in *gats* there is a close following of the moulds of *dhrupad, kheyal* and *thumri*.

Lack of a textual substratum obviously implies lack of progressions like *bol-alap, bol-tan* and *sargam*. Otherwise, the mode of presentation of *raga* always includes *alap, tan* and *layakari* (rythmic combinations).

Parallel to *bada* and *chota kheyals* there are two kinds of *gats:* one which is slow and grave *(vilambit)* well suited for *alap* and sombre development of melody, and another quicker and silvery in mood *(drut)*. Particularly for *sitar* these are often called *Maseetkhani gats* and *Razakhani gats,* respectively.

The influence on instruments of vocal music which, in India, is generally considered the acme of this art, has gained considerably in recent times. A few generations ago, instrumental rendering, specially *sitar* and *sarod,* had a peculiar characteristic manner which relied on the basic potentialities of the instrument. More recently, a style leaning heavily on vocal technicalities—what is now called the *gayaki* (vocal) approach—has become popular. The various graces, trills and glides employed by a singer are produced on the instrument so that a close semblance to human voice is created.

This close imitation and adherence to the voice has been there, and still is present, in Carnatic music. Here no special compositions for instruments exist. It is a *varnam,* a *kriti* or *padam* that is played, the audience being familiar with the words of most of them. The exposition of *raga* and sectional arrangements are as in singing, including even *neraval* and *kalpana svara*. In the improvizational parts, all the peculiarities of the instruments come out but the composition is a song and the style is vocal. There are some *banis* (schools)—for instance, the *veena* playing in Karnataka and Andhra—which have departed, to some extent, from imitations of the voice; the late Seshanna of Mysore city was an outstanding exponent of this school. Also, the current approach in South India is towards developing styles which are slowly loosening the grip of the voice and the trend seems opposite to that in North India.

While we have discussed at length various kinds of compositions or closed forms, it is worth pausing and enquiring into the status of 'composition' in Indian music.

It is necessary to distinguish between *raga* and musical form. A *raga* is a melodic concept and has a traditionally defined grammar. As we saw earlier, it is akin to a language. A musical form, on the other hand, is a composition, free or bound, in a *raga*. It is possible to have many kinds of compositions in a *raga;* conversely any type of composition is generally possible in a variety of *ragas*. Again the analogy to language is useful here. Just as we can have an epic, a sonnet or a lyric in a language so can we have *alap,* a *kheyal,* a *tarana* and so on in a *raga*.

The use of the word 'composition', has created a little misunderstanding, particularly when compared to a Western musical composition. In Western music a composition has the following characteristics: it is composed beforehand and performed later; a composer has the time and opportunity to alter and revise his work and bring it to a state satisfying to himself; and he then puts it down in the form of a score (notation); it is later rehearsed by the players, under the direction of a conductor and even the final performance is controlled by his baton. Such music, therefore, more or less partakes of the nature of a drama: there is the writer who writes the play, the actors rehearse it and put it on board under the supervision of the director and producer. What we hear and see in both cases are well thought out and premeditated pieces of art. Improvization is minimum and the skill lies in small but very important adjuncts of tone, volume and speed.

Indian music is different from this, essentially. It is individual to the highest degree and the finest art lies in a severe combination of a spontaneity of improvization and a strict control of grammar. What the Indian musician is trained in are basically three areas: (i) grammar of *raga* and *tala*; he has to learn and practise on a number of such patterns and be aware of their subtle but significant differences; (2) technical skill in manipulating the medium-voice or instrument and (3) a very sensitive understanding of the mood of the *raga* and *tala*. A high proficiency in and a deep comprehension of all the three is indeed rare. But, given even these three, there is always the most difficult stage: that of instantaneous creation with no time for revision. For, while a musician receives training in grammar and skill, gets a guidance on the mood and even meditates *(sadhana)* on it, all these may not be sufficient to release him from the inhibitions of the conscious mind in actual performance. Hence, it is that really great artists are rare, as performers, and most concerts are virtuoso demonstrations, of a very high order, perhaps, with flashes of creativity.

In such a context what is the position of a closed form—a composition—in classical music? First, of course, is the fact of its inherent merit as a song or *gat*. In a song the combination of words and music, if well knit, have their own aesthetic appeal and value. A *kriti* of Tyagaraja, a *devara nama* of Purandaradasa or a song by Rabindranath Tagore is a thing of great beauty in itself. As songs of devotion, love and literary excellence they have their distinct place in Indian music. But as a part of *raga* elaboration, a composition has to have certain other requirements. The important condition is that it should be amenable to growth and variation both in melody and rhythm. That is, it should be so constructed that a musician gets the opportunity to improvise on it with *tans, bol-tans, Sargam, neraval* and other lines of expansion. However, a *dhrupad* is not suitable both in its tonal range and rhythmic setting for development as a *kheyal;* conversely a *kheyal's* melodic line and temporal movement are too loose to admit a severe *dhrupadic* design. A sombre and epic song of Muthuswami Dikshitar precludes a lyrical outburst which is nearer the spirit of Tyagaraja. Actually, it is only in the *alap, jod, tanam* etc. that the performer is almost completely free. As soon as the song or *gat* starts, he has to conform to its *tala* and weave the musical design within its framework, never going out of tempo or *tala*. Also, a good artiste makes even his *raga* elaboration (within the composition) follow, as far as possible, the pattern of the song or *gat*. For example, a phrase incorporated in a closed form of rhythm 2+3+2+3 will be different from one in 2+2+2+2. A satisfactory progression is that while, taking the scheme of the *prabandha* as a basis, introduces variations, makes the composed phrases grow, creates contrasts but returns to the basic line with a fine resolution of musical completeness. Thus, a composition sets guidelines for a balanced presentation of *raga* and *tala*.

During the course of the developments on a song, often the meaning of the text gets mutilated, sometimes beyond recognition. This is generally excused, for in a *dhrupad,* a *kheyal,* and a *pallavi* (specially in variations like *bol-tan* and *neraval*) the music is more important than the lexical meaning of the song. But in *thumri, bhajan, padam* or *javali,* this will be inexcusable, because the beauty of such forms lies in the close synthesis of semantic content and musical mood.

A composer is known as *vaggeyakara.* The word is derived from three others *vak* (word), *geya* (song) *kara* (one who makes). As the term shows, a composer must be a master of word and music. If, on the other hand, a person writes only the libretto of a song, he is a *matukara (matu-*word or speech); if he provides the music to a given poem, he is a *dhatukara (dhatu-*score, musical part of a song). But a *vaggeyakara* composes both the poem and music—that is, he creates a complete song. The degree of command of the various branches of knowledge necessary for a composer is such that not everyone can attain this status. For the libretto *(text-matu)* must be well in conformity with the accepted grammar of the language; the composer is expected to have a profound lexical equipment—for otherwise, he cannot build in synonyms and multiple meanings so characteristic of Indian languages; obviously he should be a master of prosody and aesthetics *(rasa);* to a deep understanding of *raga* and *tala* must also be added a great familiarity with ancient and contemporary musical forms and contents.

What then is a good song? Purandaradasa says, "There should be rhythm, there should be melody, but there should be peace. There should be metre and prosody, there should be no confusion; but there should be the love of the Lord in the song". Tyagaraja exclaims, "Who is the great musician who can please Thee with drum and cymbal? Who is there who can create a song with accuracy of tone, with correctness of prosody, replete with the wisdom of the scriptures, with the nine *rasas* and true devotion."

Before closing this chapter one may look into two important changes in the social context of music.

The question of *gharana* is an important aspect of music—whether vocal or instrumental. This is particularly so in Hindustani music, for Carnatic music, though generally recognizing the *banis,* is not so insistent on such clear cut distinctions. Time was when the institution of *gharana* was sacrosanct. These *gharanas* were musical dialects and stylistic renderings originated perhaps by certain masters. North India, where Hindustani music is prevalent, is a wide extent of land and it is natural that its music has more dialects than South India. Basing himself on his own temperament, vocal capacity and musical aptitude, a great master develops a style and his descendents *(gharana)* follow him; the students trained in his family also adopt the same style. A *gharana*—'house', 'guild', 'school'—was thus born.

The tradition could be kept up mainly because of the psychological attitudes, orthodoxy and the slow means of communication. First, the disciple paid implicit obedience to the master and only then could he learn the art to any degree worth noticing. He did and had to imitate the *guru* in music, in mannerisms and habits—good as well as obnoxious. This was particularly so as learning was oral and intensely personal. Both the *guru* and *sisya* (disciple) were quite orthodox about these attitudes and it would have been sacrilegeous to cross the boundaries. Secondly, means of communication were also poorer, with lack of radio, gramophone and travelling facilities; so, a student did not have a chance to hear many different styles—and in consequence confuse himself. In fact, a generation ago a *guru* would give a chunk of his mind to his disciple if he even came to know that the student ever went to listen to a musician of another *gharana;* But, while these may appear as restrictive habits, they really resulted in excellent chiselling of musical technique and inculcation of a definite style—albeit sometimes stiff and wooden.

Today the situation is fast changing. The *guru-sisya* tradition itself is going abegging. Indeed, there are not many *gurus* worth the name, though almost every musician has started calling himself a *pandit* or an *ustad*. Present economic and social situations are not conducive to such intense relationships. There are a number of musicians who call themselves disciples of such and such a great man. But this great man is more often on his concert tour—preferably abroad—and *deigns* to visit India once a year. And that annual contact—mostly spent in public relations—is all that goes as 'teaching time'! The mental attitudes are undergoing a different orientation. The student—not having a *guru* except in name—learns from many teachers and, if he is in an institution or university, from a number of mediocre tutors or even from a text book. He has now a chance to listen to more concerts, the radio, the gramophone, the tape and so on; why, he sometimes even *learns* from them. There is also a spirit of enquiry and adventure. These have made our musicians more eclectic and catholic, for *gharanas* have ceased to have a hold on them. But this has, unfortunately, been at the cost of style and individuality.

The second aspect of *raga-tala* rendition is the concert pattern. There has grown a significant difference, affecting the artiste as well as the audience. A couple of decades ago, soirees *(mehfil, kacheri)* were most often intimate, rarely exceeding two hundred listeners, except of course big festivals. Public address system was not common. More important, usually it was an all night concert, with only one artiste (and his accompanists) performing. Therefore, the performance and its appreciation could be slow and person-to-person. Elaborate *alap,* rhythmic play and forms like *pallavi* were appreciated. But with the coming of the public address system and its increasing use, the situation is very different now. The audience runs into thousands and the connoisseur who is not common in the crowd may even shun it. Therefore, a musician now has little time for careful elaboration of melody and rhythm, but indulges in fast *tans* and at breakneck speed. A typical concert now-a-days follows generally this pattern :

A Hindustani musical evening may bill not one but, say, three or four artists for an evening; late night or whole night performances are not popular, particularly in large-cities where the problem is of conveyance. Each musician gets about half to one hour within which to squeeze, say, two *kheyals* or one *kheyal* and a *thumri* (or a *bhajan*). The order of rendition is a *vilambit (bada) kheyal* incorporating the *alap* and *tan*—less of the former and more of the latter, then the *drut (chota) kheyal,* with more *tans.* There is not much of *bol-tan* or rhythmic design and of course it is a fashion to put in a good amount of *sargam* (sol-fa) singing. If the singing is of *dhrupad,* the presentation will start with an *alap* in three sections: slow, middle and fast tempos, commencing with the lower octaves and building up to the upper. Then follows the *prabandh (bandish)* or song where emphasis is more on rhythm. Instrumental—particularly the stringed ones, for wind instruments follow more or less the pattern described above—begin with an *alap* followed by *jode* and *jhala.* Then comes the slow *gat* wherein the *alap* is again incorporated, but this time linked to the *laya* and *tala.* The faster *gat* is then played with a quick *paltas.* One very significant characteristic of specially instrumentalists, though vocalists also indulge in it, is the *tihayi:* that is, arriving exactly on to the first beat *(sam)* with a melodic-rhythmic phrase repeated thrice. The concert more often than not ends with the *raga Bhairavi.*

The Carnatic *kacheri* is patterned differently. The singer or instrumentalist will take off with a song in prayer to Lord Ganapati, the God who sees you across obstacles. Then follows a *varnam* to be succeeded by a line of *kritis.* Each of these pieces may be proceeded by a brief *alapana* to set the mood and clear voice. The musician will now perform one *raga* in detail. If he and the audience are trained *rasikas,* an elaborate *pallavi* is sung. This consists of the *alapana* (usually called just *ragam*), the *tanam* and then the *pallavi* composition proper. Often the *tanam* and the later part of the *pallavi* is performed in a *ragamalika* (garland of *ragas*) keeping the same *tala.* The libretto is the same but is sung in a series of *ragas,* the succession being arbitrary, every time with a return to the original *raga.* After this, again a few *kritis* and then lighter varieties such as *padam, javali, tillana,* devotional songs, love songs and so on. The *kacheri* comes to an end with the *mangalam* (benediction), usually set in *ragas Madhyamavati* or *Saurashtra.*

What do the accompanists do? There are at least three accompanists to the main artiste: the *tambura,* the melodic and the rhythmic.

Hindustani concerts have two *tamburas* and Carnatic one. The function is very important for, they are the bourdon tones which give the base, integrative sound and tonal backdrop. The Hindustani melodic accompaniments are the *sarangi,* and, unfortunately but very commonly, the harmonium. They follow the singer fairly faithfully but also play sometimes a few bars on their own. In a Carnatic *kacheri* the violin accompanies the voice. Besides following the voice, the violinist plays his own variations of the *alapana* and *tanam* after the vocalist has sung and before the *kriti* starts. As a matter of fact, the accompanist has much more a life of his own than in North India. There are similar differences in the drum accompaniments. While in *dhrupad* the *pakhavaji* plays the rhythmic patterns presented by the principal artiste along with him, the *tabla* accompanist now-a-days is not so competent. He usually keeps the *theka,* or the basic *tala* pattern, and after the main performer completes one or two cycles of *tala,* he launches on his own, either trying to repeat the rhythmic pattern (what is called *saval-javab*: question-answer) or more often plays his own preset and practised *bols* which have little relation to the soloist's *tala prastara.* The *mridangam* accompaniment is more to the artistic point. The player keeps a very close track of the soloist and follows him—almost simultaneously—in all *tala prastara* (rhythmic elaborations). At the end of the *pallavi* or the main rendition, he (and other percussionists) play on their own: a section which is called the *tani avartanam.*

6

Musical Instruments

THE HISTORY and evolution of the musical instruments of any culture are extremely important aspects of the music of that society. For, there exist no actual auditory records of the music of ancient human groups, at least in many areas. Scales and tunes have been nebulous, though a study of tribal and folk music alive today can yield very fruitful evidence of evolution of music. Instruments, however, are more tangible and through them, not only the music but also many facets of the material culture of an ethnic group can become clear. For instance, the wood used in making a drum, the metal of a cymbal, the hair of a bow—all these provide guides to the geographical distribution of the plants and animals available to the people of a region. Again, the migration of instruments traces the wanderings of human societies. Implements of music are also associated with various taboos: it is often seen that only some communities play certain instruments— in the villages of South India *nagasvaram* was played exclusively by barbers and in some districts of Orissa only the *Ganda* community beats the drums, while others dance and sing. Since many instruments are associated with gods, they also get their share of worship and totemistic values. Such aspects, therefore, help us in the study of the social and religious customs of a people.

In India the contribution of various cultural groups to the general pool of instruments is a very significant aspect of their history. For, the present civilization of this land is but a resultant of many a current of human activity. The tribal inhabitants of ancient times, some of whom are still with us, have their own part in this drama. It is said, for example, that the Savaras were the inventors of flute. The Aryan invaders brought with them *venu* (flute) and *veena* (harp) which, we know, were used in Vedic rituals. The *yazh* (harp) was a contribution of the Dravidian culture. Later on, the mid-western hordes which swept the country might have given us instruments— or, at least, their names—like *sarangi, tabla, sitar* and so on.

This migration has not been a one-way movement. From India instruments have travelled outside. What is known as the Greater India provides unequivocal evidence to this. We know that Indonesia has received from this subcontinent much of its ritual and culture and along with them instruments. A notable example is the *ravanahasta veena*. A bowed instrument of the western areas of India, it is, according to some scholars, the precursor of the violin. Curiously enough, the violin, after a great degree of sophistication, has come back to our concert platform, after ages.

There are at least five hundred instruments known, inclusive of those used in classical, folk and tribal music. These are generally considered as of four kinds: *tala vadya* (stringed instruments), *sushira vadya* (wind instruments), *avanaddha vadya* (covered instruments or drams) and *ghana vadya* (solid instruments). The classes correspond to the Western chordophones, aerophones, membranophones and idiophones.

Tala Vadya

The earliest stringed instruments in this country were, perhaps, the harps. Almost all of them were bow-shaped, with varying number of strings which were made of either fibre or gut. There used to be one string for each note and it was plucked either with the fingers or with a plectrum called *kona*. They were known by the generic term *veena*, with specific distinguishing names. The *chitra* had seven strings and the *vipanchi* nine; the former was played with fingers and the latter with a *kona*. The playing of such instruments was an integral part of Vedic ritual. While the priests and performers of the rites chanted the verses, the wives of the priests strummed the *kanda veena*, probably harp made of jointed reeds; *picchola* (a flute?) was also used. The ceremony was concluded with some kind of dance and some of the instrumentalists were, perhaps, even sacrificed in rites like the *Mahavrata*. The *yazh* of the ancient Tamil land was also of similar kind and description of many kinds of *yazhs* is available in old Tamil works dating from 2nd cent. A.D. Excellent representations of *veenas* and *yazhs* can be found in many sculptures and murals of bygone days. The Bharhut *stupa* (1-2 cent. B.C.), the frescoes of Ajanta (2nd-8th cent. A.D.) and many others vividly illustrate these.

Another group were of the dulcimer type. Here, a number of strings are stretched on a box of wood (resonator) to increase the volume of the sound. The best known was the *sata tantri veena*, the hundered-stringed dulcimer. This is usually identified with *santoor* still existent in Kashmir. The modern *svaramandal*, a small dulcimer, has a box of wood on which are placed about thirty metal strings. While *santoor* is played with thin sticks, *savaramandal* is strummed with the fingers.

The structure of these *veenas* seems to have been a handicap to the further development of Indian instrumental music. For, melodic lines began to become more and more intricate with greater emphasis on glides, slurs and trills. Obviously, such instruments were incapable of producing these finer tonal niceties and they gradually lost all importance. The newer trends in melodic enunciation were better suited to those instruments which could be made to produce such delicate ornamentations of *raga*. We, therefore, find that the harp-like *veena* being displaced by fingerboard instruments such as modern *veena, sitar, sarod* and so on. These not only can give the *gamakas,* but a whole *raga* can be played on even one string. That is why a single-stringed *veena* of ancient times *(ekatantri veena)* is extolled as the "original *veena*" or "*Brahma veena*" and Sarasvati, the Goddess of Learning, Herself is said to live in it.

Finger-board instruments are of various varieties, and so this class can be further subdivided into plucked and bowed. Each subclass is again of two kinds: fretted and non-fretted.

The simplest of plucked instruments we now have are *ek tar, tuntune* and *tamboora.* All these are only drones: that is, they are used to give merely the basic notes *Sa, Pa* and *Ma* (Doh, Sol and Fa) which form the foundation of melody. No *raga* is actually played on them. The *ek tar* and *tuntune* are ubiquitous folk instruments and the village mendicant is a familiar figure, with his unassuming accompaniment and a ballad on his lips. Both these instruments have only one string of metal (*ek*-one, *tar*-string). It runs along a bamboo rod which is fixed to a gourd or small wooden vessel, on which is a thin bridge of wood.

The modern *tamboora* consists of a large gourd (or a wooden bowl, as in the South Indian variety) almost hemispherical in shape, acting as a resonator. The top of this is covered with a fairly flat and thin plate of wood. The upper end of the bowl bears a small neck to which is attached a long hollow stem. On the flat surface of the resonator rests a wide bridge made of ivory, horn or wood. Over this pass four metal strings tuned to *Pa* (or *Ma) Sa, Sa, Sa* (Sol or Fa, Doh, Doh, Doh). The pair in the centre are in the middle octave, the normal *Sa* of the singer. The *Pa* (or *Ma)* and the last *Sa* are in the lower register or *mandra sthayi.* A very important part of the instrument, though the most inconspicuous, is the thread under the wires on the bridge. This, called the *jeevan* or *javari,* when placed in the proper position, gives the tone an extraordinary richness.

The better known fretted instruments are *sitar, been* (sometimes known as *Rudra veena)* of North India and *veena (Saraswati veena)* of South India.

Sitar: The word *'sitar'* is usually derived from *seh-tar* which in Persian means three strings. Amir Khusro (13th cent.) is often credited with the invention of this lute. But there is no evidence anywhere, either in his own writings or in those of his near contemporaries, to substantiate this. It is possible that *sitar* is a modified version of indigenous fretted lutes depicted in sculptures from about the 12th cent.

The instrument is made entirely of wood and is a long-necked lute. At the lower end is a gourd which is the sound-box. From this projects a neck extending into a long finger-board which may often bear a small gourd at the upper end acting as secondary resonator. On the finger-board curved frets of metal are tied by means of gut at proper places to suit the scale of the *raga* to be played.

There are five metallic strings passing over a wide bridge on the cover of the lower resonator, and along the finger-board. They are tuned as *Ma, Sa, Pa, Sa, Pa* (Fa, Doh, Sol, Doh, Sol) of lower octaves. While these are used for playing the melody, there are two more, called *chikari,* tuned to *Sa* (Doh), middle and upper registers, used as drone and for playing the progression, *jhala.* Underneath the frets runs a set of thin wires (*tarab*) tuned to the *raga* being played. Whenever a note is struck on the main upper string, the *tarab* wire tuned to this note begins to vibrate, thus acting as a sympathetic vibrator; this extra resonance enriches the sound of the instrument. The addition of *tarab* is typical of many concert and folk stringed instruments of North India, curiously enough absent in the South, except in *gottuvadyam.*

Been is simple in construction. It has two gourds, uncut and whole unlike in *sitar,* which help in increasing the volume of sound. On these is affixed a bambo or sometimes a wooden tube which is the finger-board (*dandi*). This bears a number of frets, fixed to the bamboo tube by means of wax, making them immovable. Such fixed frets are in contrast to those of *sitar* where they can be slid up and down to suit the *raga.* That is why their number is greater in *been* than in *sitar.* Another difference is that in *been* the frets are thin edges, whereas in *sitar* they are wider and convex. Four strings of metal usually tuned as *Sa, Pa, Sa, Pa* (Doh, Sol, Doh, Sol) are stretched over a wide bridge which is fixed at the lower end of the *dandi.* Besides these main wires on which the actual melody is played, there are four auxiliary ones — three on one side and one on the other. Tuned to *Sa, Pa, Sa,* (Doh, Sol, Doh) and *Sa* (Doh), they form the drone — the basic notes — and also are employed for playing *jhala. Been* is held across the body in diagonal manner, with the upper gourd resting on the shoulder. Venerable though the instrument is, it is not very popular as it does not have quicksilver quality of *sitar* but is ponderous. *Been* is closely associated with the *dhrupad* style and the music played on it is heavy.

The folk counterpart of *been* is *kinnari,* an ancient instrument found in western and southern parts of the country. It is constructed like *been;* however, there are sometimes three gourds instead of two. Incidentally, this word *kinnari* is an interesting one, as this term is used for three types of instruments: the plucked type which was just mentioned, a bowed kind of folk 'violin' in South India and a lyre of central Asia. It may be of interest to note that the Bible talks of a *kinorrah* which, perhaps, was a lyre.

Veena of South India (also known sometimes as *Sarasvati veena*) is different from *been* by being made entirely of wood. The long hollow finger-board is also of wood, though separately made and attached to the neck. But in special cases, the whole instrument is carved out of one log of wood; such a lute is called *ekanda veena.* This kind of *veena* is supposed to be of very high quality and is greatly valued. At the farther end of the finger-board and under it there is another gourd acting as an extra resonator. The frets of metal are broader than in *been* and are fixed by means of wax. The strings of metal, four in number, pass over a wide bridge and are tuned as *Sa, Pa, Sa, Pa* (Doh, Sol, Doh, Sol). Besides these, there are three drone strings passing over an auxillary bridge of metal; they are tuned to *Sa, Pa, Sa* and used both as a drone and for giving the *tala.*

Closely similar to the above but without frets are *vichitra veena* of North India and *gottuvadyam* of the southern parts of the country. The former is akin to *rudra been* and the latter to *Sarasvati veena,* both in construction and manner of plucking. A ball or a small cylinder of glass (or hard ebony wood) is slid along the wires to play the melody. The structure and technique of such instruments place severe handicaps on the player. The absence of frets is itself a difficulty; but to adjust the pressure of the *kodu* or *batta* (the slider) is an extremely delicate process and even the slightest change in pressure introduces deviations in pitch. It is therefore rare to find really competent players of these instruments.

Sarod is another instrument without frets and is very much like *rabab* of mid-western and central Asia. It has a small and deep body of wood which projects into a short neck and finger-board. The body is covered with parchment and the board with a steel plate. A small bowl of metal is screwed to the farther end of the finger-board into its lower side. Unlike *sitar, been* and *veena, sarod* has a narrow bridge, like in a violin. The melody strings are six, tuned as *Ma, Sa, Pa, Sa, Pa, Sa* (Fa, Doh, Sol, Doh, Sol, Doh) of lower octaves. The strings are plucked with a 'triangular' piece of wood held in one hand while the other hand is employed for pressing the strings onto the board. As in *sitar* there is a pair of drone strings *(chikari)* and a *tarab.* Lutes of this kind appear quite early in the history of Indian instruments as can be seen in the frescoes of Ajanta (2nd-8th cent. A.D.), and the remains of the Buddhist city, Nagarjunakonda (2nd cent. A.D.), Amaravati (1st B.C.-2nd cent. A.D.) and many others.

Surprisingly, bowed instruments have not risen to the same standing in concerts as the plucked ones. Till very recently they have been *geetanuga,* that is, accompaniment to singing. While *sarangi* in the North is still so (though one does come across a solo recital), the violin in the South (and even in North India) has slowly emerged as a solo instrument. In folk and tribal music, however, they are quite ubiquitous. *Ravanahasta veena,* for instance, has come to us from centuries and is popular in Western India even today. *Pena* of Assam, *kinnari* of South India and *banam* of Orissa are some of the common fiddles that one comes across. The folk *sarangi* of North-Western India has been known from at least the 13th century and in its sophisticated form has been admitted to the concert platform. The body of the instrument is hollowed out of wood, the resonator being covered with skin and the finger-board with wood. It is held as an inverted violin. The bow is a heavy one and different in shape and construction than that of a violin. The gut strings are three, and are tuned to *Sa, Pa, Sa* (Doh, Sol, Doh) in the lower octave. They are not stopped with the balls of the fingers but by sliding the nails along the side. A set of *tarab* passes under the main strings.

Another bowed instrument popular in North India is the *dilruba.* In Bengal, there is a similar instrument called the *esraj.* In both the cases the sound box is like that of *sarangi.* But the finger-board is much longer and bears frets. Unlike in *sarangi,* the strings are pressed with the balls of the fingers as in the violin, *veena* or *sitar.* The main strings are four tuned to *Ma, Sa, Pa, Sa.* Besides, there is a pair of drone strings and a *tarab,* all of metal.

Avanaddha Vadya

Drums are instruments, hollow and covered with skin (hence the term *avanaddha*) and used in music and dance as rhythmic accompaniments. But all drums are not always put to musical uses. For example, the slit-drums of Assam, common in many areas and to tribes, are hollow boat shaped wooden implements kept on the ground and beaten. We cannot really call these drums as usually understood. Also, drums have not always been musical in function. The *ranabheri* was a martial instrument; there are also the signalling drums of Africa, whereon codes are tattooed out — a precursor of the Morse code! The village announcer with his strident *daff* is a familiar figure to all of us.

The musical uses of drums start, however, with primitive dance-music rites and rituals. Even today the great variety of folk drums is *nrityanuga*, i.e., accompaniments to dance. Of course, in primitive and folk levels, dance and music are inseparable and because of the ritualistic association in early human societies *avanaddha vadyas* have had magical value. "The drum is indispensable in primitive life; no instrument has so many ritual tasks, no instrument is held more sacred". The sacred symbolism of *damaru* of Lord Siva is profound to the highest degree. Once the Lord was dancing in ecstacy on Mount Kailas. Great sages gathered round the Divine Dancer, entranced and spellbound. When the dance came to an end, they prostrated at His feet and begged that the knowledge of the Sound be made available to humans. He then took up His *damaru* and played on it fourteen times, giving birth to the fourteen aphorisms of grammar which also are the base of all music.

Pushkara is the ancient Sanskrit word for the drum. This is how the instrument came to be invented: Once the Sage Svati went to fetch water from a lake (*pushkara* also means a lake or pond) near his abode. Just then Indra (Pakasasana) sent torrential rains onto the earth. Svati listened deeply to the patter — sweet and pleasing — of the rain drops on the lotus leaves (*pushkara* again means blue lotus). With the sounds still ringing in his ears, he returned to the hermitage. Then he made *mridanga* and *pushkaras* such as *panava* and *dardura*, with the assistance of Visvakarma, the godly craftsman. On seeing *dundubhi* he fashioned *muraja* and other drums.

Mridanga type of instruments are to be found in terracota figurines of the Indus Valley civilization, according to some. Vedic literature refers to *bhumi dundubhi, panava* and such others. The former was, perhaps, the most ancient. It comprised a pit in the ground covered with skin which was beaten. Drums made of earth appear later in the history of musical instruments; but, being fragile, they have largely given place to wooden ones. These latter come next in the field and even today, *pakhavaj, mridang* and *tabla* are made of wood.

Avanaddha vadyas are of various types and they have been classified on the basis of their position of play, shapes and structure. For example, *urdhvaka, ankya* and *alingya* are three kinds, different by the way they are placed when playing. *Urdhvaka* drums are held vertically — *chenda* of Kerala, *tabla, nagara* and so on. *Ankya* are those that are kept horizontally; *dholak, pakhavaj, mridang, khol* and similar *pushkaras* are of this category. *Alingya* are 'embraced'; that is — are held under one arm and struck with the other, like *timila* of Kerala.

Drums are also differentiated as barrel and frame; in other words, closed and open. Closed ones are those in which the hollow body is covered, either at one end or both ends by membrane. Of the former kind are *tabla, bayan, nagara, ghumar.* Of the latter type are *mridanga, pakhavaj, dholak, damaru,* etc. An open drum, on the other hand, consists of a circular frame covered with skin on one side; for instance, *daff, khanjira* and similar tambourines.

Mridanga (Pakhavaj): The word *mridang* itself suggests an earthern structure (*mrt*-earth, clay, *anga*-body). And we know that a number of drums are made of burnt clay; even *dagga* used in North Indian concert music is often earthen. However, according to some, *mridanga* was so called not because of its earthen body but because of the clay paste which was applied to the leather surface. But in current practice a blackish mixture of manganese or iron dust called *syahi* (Hindi) or *soru* (Tamil) is affixed to the beaten surface of the instrument.

Mridanga is one of the most ancient drums of India. In its present form, it is a barrel-shaped wooden body, bulging in the middle and tapering towards the ends. The membrane forming the drum face is complex—that is, it is not one single layer of skin, but a set of two or more suitably cut circular pieces glued together. The two faces are held to the body by means of plaits and with each other by a strap of leather passing through the plaits. Underneath the braces are placed cylindrical wooden blocks (usually eight) which are employed for tuning. Finer tuning is done by striking the plaits with a hammer. The wooden cylinders are used only in the North Indian variety, commonly called *pakhavaj;* South Indian *mridangam* does not have these.

A very interesting part of Indian drums is the loading of the leather surfaces. This was known as *vilepana* in older Sanskrit works. Nowadays the popular word is *syahi* in North India and *soru* in South India. Generally, it is the right face that carries a permanent loading. *Vilepana* makes the sound of the instrument musical and eliminates the noisy quality so characteristic of plain leather drums like *daff,* tambourine and even the kettle drum. The left surface is not fixed with this kind of paste permanently; but, just before the time of actual playing soft dough mixed with water is stuck to it.

Mridangam is still the premier percussion instrument in Carnatic music. However, *Pakhavaj,* used for accompanying *dhrupad* and *been,* is slowly going out of vogue and has given place to *tabla.*

Tabla : No one seems to know the correct history of *tabla.* There has been a controversy as to whether it is an indigenous instrument or an import from the Arabic and Persian areas. Like many other controversial topics its 'invention' is credited to Amir Khusro and Muslim culture, connecting it with the word *table,* a Persian drum. While this may or may not be really so, we have sufficient evidence to show that *tabla* might have had a local and pre-Muslim origin. Sculptures of pairs of vertically placed drums appear very early (6th-7th cent. A.D.) and the application of paste on drum faces is also an old practice as can be seen in the *pushkaras* depicted in Ajanta. Even as early as Bharata's *Natyasastra* the technique of applying the load *(vilepana)* was well known. It is possible that the instrument itself is Indian and only the word *tabla* is foreign. However, a legend is always there; and this particular one ascribes the avention of *tabla* to one Sudhar Khan Dhadi, said to be a contemporary of Akbar. There was, so the story goes, a *pakhavaji* called Bhagavandas. Sudhar Khan and Bhagavandas were professional rivals and competitors. Having failed to defeat the *pakhavaji,* Dhadi in a fit of understandable temper dashed his *pakhavaj* down. It broke into two pieces and he, then, made these into *tabla* and *bayan (dagga).* Quite a convenient accident.

While *mridanga* and *pakhavaj* are single drums, covered on both faces, *tabla* is really a pair of drums—one like a coffee cup and the other like a tea cup. Though the pair is together called *tabla,* strictly speaking *tabla* is one of the set of two, the other being *dagga (or duggi); dagga* is also often referred to as *bayan,* meaning the left drum. While the right one *(tabla)* has a wooden body with a covering of leather on the top, *dagga* is made of metal or burnt clay. The stretching of the leather in both is as in *pakhavaj.* The former can be tuned accurately, but *bayan* has an indefinite pitch, though it is often assumed that it is tuned to an octave lower than *tabla.* Also the loading of the black paste is centric in *tabla* and eccentric in *dagga.* Both the drums are kept erect on the ground and played with the fingers. Unlike *mridanga, tabla* has a lighter and sweeter sound; it is, therefore, well suited for accompanying *kheyal, thumri* etc. and softer instruments like *sitar, sarod* and so on.

Just as there are *kheyal gharanas* there are schools (or *baj*) of *tabla.* Traditionally, the Delhi *gharana* is said to be the mother of all later ones. The players of this group use the rim of the *tabla* more than the centre, the first and middle finger more than other combinations, the sounds thus being delicate; their patterns are also smaller. The *Ajrada gharana,* called so after the town of that name where the originator of this style lived, while leaning on the Delhi one, uses combinations with heavier left handed strokes and revels in odd rhythms. The other major branch is the *poorab* or eastern one which comprises styles known as the *Lucknowi baj, Banarasi baj* and *Farrukhabadi baj.* These have been highly influenced by *pakhawaj* and exhibit some of its characteristics: open sounds, flat strokes and using the central parts of the drums more. There is one more: the Punjab *gharana* which does not trace itself to Delhi but claims a separate origin and development. The style relies much on the *pakhawaj,* thus using heavy sounds and long patterns.

The instruments described so far are all used in concerts. There are, of course, the folk and tribal counterparts of these. *Dholak, khol, pung* and such other drums are of the barrel type; *nagara, tamuku, tasa* and so on are drums more or less cup-shaped and covered with leather on one side.

Sushira Vadya

These are instruments in which sound is produced by the vibration of air columns. Being hollow tubes, with or without appendages, they have been termed as *sushira* (hollow) *vadya* (instrument).

Of the concert instruments, the most important are flutes, particularly the cross flute (the one held across the face) and the *mukha veena* family (*shehnai* and *nagasvaram*).

Flute : One of the commonest of musical instruments of the world, the flute is also one of the most ancient. It is a part of every musical system we know of, from the most primitive people to the most sophisticated civilizations. Not only so, its form is more or less the same throughout the world and has remained unaltered during the course of human history.

Most commonly, the flute is made of bamboo. The bamboo used to make the instrument should be straight, clean, smooth and free from cracks. It should be neither too young nor too old. Flutes are also made of red sandal wood, *khadira* wood (*Acasia catechu*), black wood and cane; even ivory, ebonite, bronze, brass, silver and gold have been used. The normal diameter of the instrument is two centimeters, though wider ones are also sometimes employed. The monumental work on music, *Sangeeta Ratnakara* of Sarangadeva, written in the 13th century lists eighteen kinds of flutes, according to the distances between the blow hole and the first finger hole — the distances varying from 2 ½ cm. to 45 cm.

The commonly used material for making flutes being wood, it is obvious that it gets decayed easily. One does not, therefore, expect to find ordinary flutes in ancient excavations. However, flutes of bone, clay and metal can remain without disintegration for ages. Thus, no ancient sites in India have yielded flutes of wood. But clay whistles have been found in the Indus Valley town of Mohenjodaro (3000 B.C.). This is, perhaps, the earliest evidence of a wind instrument in our country, of pre-Vedic times.

Earlier and later Vedic texts refer to flute as *venu*. It was used as an accompaniment to Vedic recitations along with *veena* (harp). These sources also refer to a kind of flute called *tunava* employed during sacrifices. *Nadi* was another variety, probably made of reed, played to propitiate Yama, the Lord of Death. Not only was it an important instrument in religious ceremonies, but the flutist was one of the victims of human sacrifice in *Purushamedha yajna* ritual.

The flute has thus been known from very ancient times in India, and is one of the most widely distributed instruments in this country, called by various names: *venu, vamsi, bansi, bansuri, murali* and so on in North India; in South India it usually goes under the names *pillankuzhal* (Tamil), *pillanagrovi* (Telugu), *Kolalu* (Kannada), etc.

The transverse flute is the most common kind, very extensively met with. It is held across the face of the player. Flutes in the South are generally short. In the North, however, longer ones are used for playing *alap* and sometimes shorter ones for faster passages.

Unlike the transverse flute, in the beak-flute air is not blown directly into the hollow of the instrument. At one end of the tube there is a slightly conical tapering with an opening into which air is blown. This mouth-piece is known as the fipple, and hence such a flute is called the fipple flute or the flageolet. While there is no special Indian name for this type, it is yet very ubiquitous. However, it is rarely seen in concerts and is more a folk instrument.

An interesting variety of such beak-flutes is the *algoza,* a double pipe. Actually this instrument is quite old in India, for it has been depicted even in the Sanchi *stupa* (circa I[st] cent., B.C.), showing a soldier (?), most probably a foreigner, playing it. The instrument is itself a set of two flutes of the beak type. They are either tied together tightly as one piece or the two may be held together loosely with the hands. The player blows into both simultaneously; generally one of them serves as a drone and the other is used for playing the melody.

Comparable only to *veena* of Sarasvati and *damaru* of Siva, the flute has always held, for an Indian, a mystic fascination. For it is the call of Lord Krishna to his beloved Radha. She is the human soul longing for union with the Lord. And Krishna is the Adored, for ever beckoning to the Soul of Man.

His call is not merely the call of the lover to the *gopis* (milk maids), but the divine invitation to everyone. The soul of man responds:

> "Still must I like a homeless bird
> Wander, forsaking all;
> The earthly loves and worldly lures
> That held my life in thrall,
> And follow, follow, answering
> The magical flute-call".*

Mukhaveena: While *venu,* the flute, is as old as the Vedas, the *mukhaveena* family comprising *mukhaveena, nagasvara, ottu, shehnai* and *sundri* is definitely of much later origin, though the group is widely distributed throughout the country.

Mukhaveena, a smaller variety of *nagasvara* is referred to by the Telugu poet Palkuriki Somanantha who lived in 12th-13th century. *Nagasvara* is mentioned in the Telugu poem *Skanda puranam,* Srinatha's *Kreedabhiraman* (14th cent.) and Ahobala's *Sangeeta parijata* (17th cent.).

Even on examining such material carefully, it is not easy to conclude that such references pertain to the wood wind instruments we now know of. For example, while *mukhaveena* is a double-reed wood pipe in the South, it is described by the author of *Sangeeta sara* (18th cent.) as a small bamboo tube wound round with *bhoorja* leaves. Similarly, *nagasvara (nagasara)* may mean both the present day concert instrument of Carnatic music as well as the snake charmers' *pungi (mahudi, been,* etc.). Indeed, the name *nagasvaram* itself points to association with the snake charmer: *naga* = snake, *svara* = sound, note, music.

Shehnai is usually taken to be an imported instrument from the Middle East. Its Persian name is said to be *surnai,* changed to *shehnai* in India. The older Mongolian variety traced to India is also known as *surnai.* While the author of *Sangeeta sara* mentions an instrument *sunari* very much like a *shehnai,* perhaps it was the same as *sundri,* a diminutive double-reed pipe of Maharashtra.

All the instruments of this family have the same basic structure and technique of playing, their differences lying mostly in their sizes and certain minor details. The functional parts are two:

---

*Sarojini Naidu, *The Sceptred Flute,* p. 161. Kitabistan, 1946.

The reeds: These are two small flat pieces of reed held together leaving a small gap between them. The pair is fixed to the tube of the instrument either directly or by means of a metallic staple.

The tube: This is the main body of the instrument and acts as a resonator. It is more or less conical in shape, narrow near the blowing end and opening out gradually. Usually there is a 'bell' of metal at the farther end. The tube is generally of wood, but may be of metal also. *Nagasvaras* of silver, gold and even soapstone are known.

The tube bears seven holes used for playing the melody by closing or opening them. The Indian *mukhaveenas* do not have keys, unlike the Western oboes; for such mechanical arrangement cannot produce the finer *srutis* and *gamakas,* so essential to our music.

This group of instruments have generally been outdoor ones. Almost every village in South India has the *nayyandi melam* (ensemble) of which *mukhaveena* is the leader. Indeed the word *melam,* which strictly means an ensemble, has come to refer to *mukhaveena* and *nagasvara.* No temple or marriage procession can go without *nagasvara* or *shehnai,* for they are omens of auspicious beginning. Naturally, such uses have made them loud and shrill; but they have now been taken to concerts also, with changing techniques.

Other wind instruments found everywhere in the country are *sankh* (conch) and trumpets like *turahi, narsing, ekkalam, kombu* (horn) and so on. None of these have ever come to be used in sophisticated music; but they have been instruments of announcement of battle and victory. Of course, they form an important part in religious processions and the conch is even a sacred symbol of Lord Vishnu.

Ghana Vadya

The idiophones, though, perhaps, the earliest of instruments, have remained at comparatively undeveloped stages to this day. They are more rhythm beaters, suitable to folk music and dance: pots and pans, bells and jingles, rods and sticks — in fact, anything from which sound can be elicited— finds a place there. In art music, however, there are two instruments of some prominence — *ghatam* and *jaltarang.*

Ghatam is just what the word means—an earthen pot and nothing more. While it is a folk instrument in some areas like Kashmir where it is known as *noot, ghatam* is 'respectable' and admitted to concerts in South

India. The pot, made of special clay and carefully baked, is held with its mouth resting on the belly of the player and tapped on its surface with fingers. Though humble in appearance it can easily produce an astounding variety of sounds.

Jaltarang is a set of porcelain cups of different sizes filled with varying amounts of water. The size of the cup and the quantity of water in it determine its pitch. Such water-filled bowls, one for each note, are arranged in a semicircle; the player sits in the centre of this semicircle and plays on the cups with a bamboo stick in each hand.

The Indian Orchestra

There has often been a question whether India ever had an orchestra. If by orchestra we mean harmony and all its implications, it is doubtful if we ever had one. Certainly, there were instrumental groups known as *kutapa* in Sanskrit and *melam* in South India. Bharata in his *Natya Sastra* describes in detail the arrangements of instruments in *Kutapa*, when and what it should play and so on. Even today *nayyandi melam* in the villages of South India, the *pancha vadya* (five instruments) ensemble of Kerala and Orissa are common and popular. But the sophisticated music of the country has, till very recently, not admitted an orchestra and harmonization. The *vadya vrinda* (instrumental group) heard on the radio is still to mature. There is one area, however, which has taken to orchestration in a big way—the films. Not inhibited by the rigours of tradition, musicians in films have harmonized both classical and folk music—and even lifted unabashed whole pieces from jazz and blues. While such art may not be acceptable to many, it has, no doubt, brought in a new dimension of expression to Indian music.

7

Folk and Traditional Music

IT IS USUAL to distinguish between classical (or art) and folk music. But a definition of distinction between the two has not been made so far, so that no clear line can be drawn demarcating the boundaries. There are always forms like *keertan* of Bengal, *abhang* of Maharashtra and *padam* of Andhra which are set in sophisticated moulds, but yet are not considered strictly 'classical'.

A reasonable statement that can be made of folk music is that it has no conscious grammar, even if it is a grammar which changes historically like classical music. It has no consciously guided history which controls its growth. Classical music, on the other hand, has a structure which is accepted as more or less definite and inviolable, though this is really a questionable assumption. A *raga,* a *tala,* a *dhrupad* or a *varnam* is fabricated as if it can suffer no major change in its form. A folk song, for instance, a *lali pata* (a lullaby from Andhra), has a 'definite' form in music and even in text; but the singer does not intentionally follow a grammar: she goes along the way of social tradition, without enquiry (which, obviously, would only mar the beauty of the music). Such music is not a product of conservetoires!

The most widely accepted definition of a folk song is that it has no known authorship. We do not know who 'wrote' its text and who 'composed' its music, if these two things are separately done at all in a folk song. A *baul* (a mystic ministrel of Bengal) was once asked why "no effort was made to preserve the names of the composers of their songs". The elderly *baul,* pointing first to the full river where boats were passing under sail and then to the almost dry canal where boats stood on the mud, answered, "Do the boats under full sail leave any trace of their passage? The track of the boat being pushed along the canal is marked plainly in the mud. Which is the simpler and more natural way? Ours is the simple way. The leaving of footprints is artificial and unimportant". This anonymity of authorship has always been considered to be of prime importance for a folk song. But it is not always possible to accept such a *sine qua non*. The *padams* of Bhadrachala Ramadas, the *devaranamas* of *dasas* of Karnatak, the *bhajans* of Kabir, the *abhangas* of Eknath and Tukaram of Maharashtra — all these have entered the homes and hearts of untrained folk. They are often sung to tunes which can scarcely be called 'classical'. Some of them have even become lullabys and play-songs for children. Yet sometimes the authorship of these does come to light; we could then not remove them from the class of folk music, for their music is still simple without intended and planned structure. Again, no one knows, with rare exceptions, the 'originators' of *ragas* and *talas*. Yet this ignorance about their sources does not make them folk music.

The greatest significant quality of folk music is its social relation. Art music, on the contrary, has often no social function other than aesthetic satisfaction, if not mere entertainment. *Ragas* and *talas,* for example, have no connection with sowing, reaping, war, marriage, childbirth and so on. In contrast, folk songs have intimate associations with such group or individual activities. It is, therefore, easy to describe them in terms of functional categories.

The most generalized life of the village is its proximity and dependence on nature and its bounty. An office goer in a metropolis or a factory worker has very little knowledge of the effects of rain or sun on his life—except that he may have to take out his raincoat, if he does not want his clothes to be spoilt. A tiller in the field (or a hunter in the woods) is deeply in communion with the stars, the clouds, the river and the trees; they tell him when to sow, when to reap, and when the fish will be in plenty. Nature is both the bountiful mother and the terrible scourge. So he sings in praise of Her and begs for Her mercy. She is beautiful but She can be ugly. Hence there are songs of *Savan* when rains come and there is a promise of plenty. But there is also the longing in the maiden's heart; a simple but lovely Tamil song runs thus:

> "*It will rain finely mother,*
> *The country will turn green, thus will it rain.*
> *Roundly, roundly will it rain.*
> *Everywhere in the world will it rain*".[1]

There is a song for every month, for every season. *Chaitra* has the *chaiti* songs and the rains have *kajri*. The *bara masa*—the songs of twelve months— are sung almost everywhere in North India and describe the clouds of *Asadh,* the rains of *Savan,* the lighting of the lamps of *Kartik,* the spring buds of *Magh,* the festival of colours of *Phalgun.* It is not mere description, but the individual becomes the rain, the river and the earth. As paddy sprouts from mother earth, the woman longs for a child in her womb:

"May the spring never forget to enter our village
O Gowang, give us rice in plenty,
O Gowang, be kind to fields and women,
O Gowang, as a woman embraces her lover,
May the earth embrace the seed".[2]

The urge to procreate calls the youth and his love to sing to each other-
of the happiness of their union, the sorrow of separation and of hopes and
expectations. A *Bihu* song of Assam goes thus:

" I shall be swan and swim in your tank
I shall be a pigeon and sit on your roof;
I shall be perspiration and enter your body,
I shall be a fly and kiss your cheek".[3]

The *Mohana Ranga* lyrics of Andhra have a delicate beauty, all their
own. The moon-struck girl sings;

"If you become the moon, my love,
I will be the light of the moon;
How close ever I will follow you.
Come, Charming Ranga,
How close ever I will follow you".[4]

The young get betrothed and wed to find fulfillment in each other.
Marriage has, therefore, to be celebrated with joy. Whether an arranged
marriage or otherwise, it is a major occasion in a person's life and the
beginning of new and great social responsibilities. Songs for such occasions
abound in every community: to welcome the groom, to decorate the bridge,
of the nuptial chamber, on 'quarrels' of the parties and so on. The Oraon
maiden in 'strange loneliness' says :

"The dove, the dove,
Calls in the hills, the hills,
I have no mother, and I cannot sleep.
I have no father, and I cannot sleep".[5]

Parental home, the sweet place of security and love, has to be left for a
stranger's and the mother-in-law's supremacy. Here is a Kannada song on
the bride's life at the in-law's:

"Mother, how can I praise my father-in-law before you?
Mother, my life is not happy.
It is like plantains artificially ripened in the basket."[6]

Rajasthan folk satara-double
barrel beak flute

Bodo flute player

Folk music on the 'Jantar' - Rajasthani folk instrument resembling the veena

Goverdhan Bhopa with Ravanhatta - a tribal instrument in which the main string as well as the bowstring are both made from hairof horse tail

Bihari folk music players

Bihari flute player

Folk musicians from Gujarat

Folk musician from Manipur

Folk performers from Mysore

Muria Folk performers from Madhya Pradesh

**Muria Folk musician
from Bastar, Distt. M.P**

**Musical Instruments of Kashmir-
Typical instruments used for Chakkari (Natu, Tumbaknari, Sarangi)**

Folk performers from Maharashtra

Folk performers from Bihar

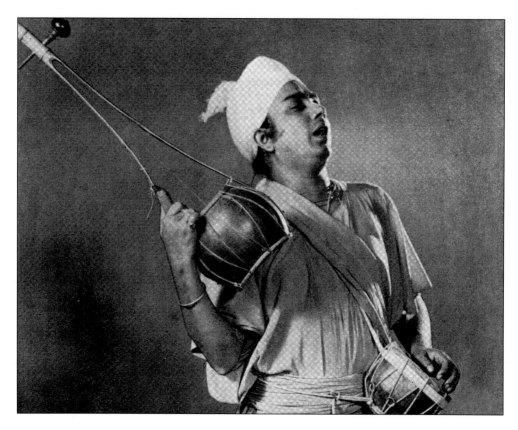

A baul singer from Bengal playing gopi yantra

The kommu of Andhra Pradesh

Marriage begets children. A daughter is not welcome, for she will leave the home and a dowry has to be paid for her marriage; but, if a son is born, he will be an additional bread-earner. This attitude is common throughout the country and has been a source of many a song.

While songs of playing with children and songs of children at play are plenty, lullabys are the finest in any society. A Gujarati mother puts her child to sleep thus:

> *"The cradle is made of gold*
> *The bells make jingling sound,*
> *Sleep, baby.*
> *Four dolls on four pillars*
> *Peacocks sit on strings,*
> *Sleep, baby."*[7]

As the child grows into an adult, he has to work for his living and the family has to be supported. The earth has to be ploughed and watered, seeds sown and corn reaped. Grain has to be taken to the market and sold. Perhaps, where the society is more primitive and food is obtained by hunting, the gods of the forest have to be propitiated. While the men toil in the field, fish in the sea or hunt in the woods, the women fetch water from the village well or a nearby stream, cook, look after the children and thresh the corn. A Pulayan of Kerala has this to say:

> *"Sitting on the stone, O crab,*
> *Move a little,*
> *From the stone, O crab,*
> *Let me plough the field, O crab,*
> *Move a little,*
> *From the stone, O crab."*[8]

Again :

> *"O pretty maiden,*
> *Where have your brothers gone?"*
> *"They are out to collect reeds."*
> *"What is the use of reeds?"*
> *"The reeds are good for making cots."*[9]

A song of the spinning wheel from Punjab complains:

> *"My spinning wheel is made of kikar wood*
> *Get me a wheel of sandal, darling,*
> *I will not spin cotton.*

I will not spin wool.
Get me silk to spin, darling.
My spinning wheel is made of kikar wood, darling,
Get me a wheel of sandal, darling."[10]

Ballads are a very important section of a people's music. They do not generally have the lyrical qualities of folk poetry as in songs instanced above. Of course, it is not necessary that they be devoid of such content. But ballads are more concerned with advancing "the statement of fact" and to "help the narrative." They are the unwritten history of the community; naturally, every people has its own heroes and heroines. Andhra's *burra katha*, Maharashtra's *povada*, the *Katta Bomman* songs of Tamil Nadu, the *pad* of Rajasthan all sing of the glories of their valorous men and women, and eulogise their successes. Fine examples are the war songs of Rajasthan which, as Tagore said, have been "created out of her blood". These poems called *doha* or *dooha* are sung by bards known as *charans*. A *charan* could be a cattle-breeder or an itinerant trader who, besides his regular profession of raising cattle and horses or selling arms, goes round singing legends of martial inspiration:

"When you reach the battle field, my love,
What will you hold superior?
Your companions are three –
A stout heart, a sharp sword and a strong hand" [11]

A large class of songs can be classified as religious and festive. The number of religious groups — from the most elemental and anthropomorphic to the most refined—are so many; and the nature and number of songs are equally varied. The village goddess, perhaps, demanding animal sacrifice, has to be pleased if the corn is to grow high, if smallpox is not to visit the hamlet. Or it may be a prayer of the finest devotion and most subtle mysticism.

Of the festival songs may be cited *chait parab* of Orissa and border areas, the music of the Spring, when groups of young men go round the village collecting money to spend on intoxicants. Singing continues throughout the night in the local shrines. Seeking the blessings of the goddess the singer exclaims:

"Victory to you, Goddess Mahamai,
Victory to you, Mother Kalika
I begin my song in your Name
Be kind and make my throat Your seat." [12]

While such are the songs of the simpler tribes, the more sophisticated have devotional music of a different order. Bengal, for instance, has *baul* and *keertan. Baul* is a wandering mendicant, detached from the turmoils of society and the songs he sings are also called *baul :*

> *"Temples and mosques conceal Your way*
> *I hear Your call and cannot come, O Lord.*
> *The Gurus and Mursheds stand barring my path."*[13]

The demarcation of folk and art or classical music in India is really vague. The kind of music which finds a place in village gatherings, temple services, rural theatres as well as in concerts has a niche of its own; and it is sung and played, very often, in definable *ragas* and *talas*. There is then a necessity to distinguish between tribal and folk music on the one hand and the 'classical' music on the other, with a third category which, for a lack of a suitable word, is sometimes called 'traditional' music. Under the last fall *keertan, tevaram, padam, abhang,* various forms of theatrical music and so on, some of which have already been described briefly earlier.

Keertans are congregational songs, both Vaishnavaite and Sakta—worshipping Lord Vishnu (Krishna) and Goddess Sakti. Of great poetic and musical beauty, they are the special features of Bengal. Of the best known composers of *keertans* may be mentioned Chandidas and Chaitanya. Similarly, the poems and lyrics of Meera, Kabir, Dadu and Tulsi have pervaded the common folk and elite throughout the Hindi-speaking areas. *Abhangs* of Eknath, Jnaneswar and Tukaram have given us in Marathi some of the finest religious poems in music that we know of. South India has *padas* of Bhadrachala Ramadas, *devaranamas* of Purandara and other *dasas,* and *vachanas* and *tevarams* of Saivite saints. The *sabads* of the Sikhs and *qavvalis* and *qalbanas* of the Muslims are also of this category, and wherever Christian influence has penetrated deeply as in Goa, Kerala and Nagaland, hymns in Western musical style, but in the local dialect, have become common.

The religious music of the people offers a very rich field for the meeting of folk and classical art. Quite a number of songs are simple tunes sung to the accompaniment of *ek-tar* (a monochord) and a *chipla* or *kartal* (clappers). Many are congregational, sung in *samaj* and *bhajana gosthi* (devotional groups); they are, therefore, of necessity uncomplicated. Though the degree of sophistication of such music makes them suspect as folk songs, neither do they have the finesse and strictness of classical music; and hence cannot strictly be considered so.

The above outline of the kinds of folk songs which one may come across in India has perforce to be sketchy; for this is a vast, ancient and variegated land. From Himalayan snows to tropical jungles, from the arid deserts of

Rajasthan to the fertile valley of the Ganga, from the stony plateau of Deccan to the sandy sea-shores of the peninsula, the terrain, the fauna, the flora and the human settlements differ multi-fold. Lives are different, social structures are different and ancestries are different. From Austroloid to Aryan, from gypsy to tribal huntsmen, ethnical groups present their own cultural patterns. There are areas which have not yet been touched by the current techno-civilization; there are also the highly congested cities with all their ugliness. Naturally, with so conglomerate a milieu, the music of the soil is also equally varied in its social relations, content and form.

The musical forms of these songs and tunes also show great differences. At the primeval levels, it is not even easy to recognize the 'musicality' of some. For instance, the shuffling 'dance' of certain Nagas is accompanied by a kind of grunt which can scarcely be called music. Yet it does sound 'musical'. So are the yells and screeches of many a folk and tribal group. These apart, there are certain types of 'recitations' called *churnikas* which are prose-songs. They are often 'sung' by bards and heralds (*bhattas* and *charanas*) in praise of kings and gods. While the music is still 'folkish', even a composer like Tyagaraja has introduced *churnikas* in his opera; for example, *Jayatu jayatu* in *Prahlada Bhakti Vijayam*.

The simplest 'music' would be, of course, of a single tone. Such monotonous sing-song was the *archika* style of reciting the Veda. Two-tone and three-tone chants were known as *gathika* and *samika*. Recitative music of this kind is found not only in these ecclesiastical psalms, but also in many songs of children and even adults: some *ovis* of Maharashtra employ only two or three notes. From such rudimentary incantations to highly developed tunes we may meet any stage and type. As in melody so in rhythm. The most elementary are the three-unit beats. But even at the tribal levels rhythm has already grown into a very intricate art. The drumming of the Santals—to give an example—though seemingly 'primitive' is extraordinarily complex. What is more, it has already got standardized mnemonics. Folk drumming of *kardi majlu* of Karnataka is another such, which only goes to show that folk music is not always simpler than classical.

What is of importance is to realize and acknowledge the fact that this music of the 'masses' is of the soil, from which the art, music of the elite has sprung and to which it has to turn again and again to obtain sustenance. We may not easily recognize the affinity of the more 'refined' *ragas* to the 'cruder' folk tunes. But one can still find their patterns there in budding form. It would be more than absurd to call some of these tunes of tribes and villages as *ragas* and their rhythms as *talas,* for they have not yet been given a grammar. Nonetheless, as we listen to a snake-charmer on his *pungi*, we cannot but connect the tune with *Nadanamakriya raga*. The common lullaby, *Bala jo jo re* in Marathi, has the nucleus of *raga Sarang*. Other patterns met with are those of *Bhoop, Bhairavi, Bilaval, Pilu, Kafi* of North India and *Kuranji, Chenjuriti, Ananda-bhairavi* of South India. Parallely, rhythmic archetypes of *Trital, Roopak, Jhumra, Adi* and *Chapu* are usual and it is from these melodies and beats that the greatest of concert music draws its life.

Songs, 1, 3, 4, 6, 7, 8, 9, 10, 11, 12, 13-quoted from D. Satyarthi, *Meet My People*, pp. 166, 186, 199, 215, 236, 209, 96, 63, 111, 160, (Chetana, 1951), and songs 2, 5 from H. Barua, *Folk Songs of India*, pp. 2, 30 (Indian Council for Cultural Relations, Delhi, 1963).

8

Mind and Music

THE INDIAN theory of emotions has been usually associated with art (specially literary) appreciation in the well-known theory of *rasa*, mainly based on what is termed sometimes as the Hindu psychology.

This psychology recognizes the role of the unconscious and racial memory (instincts) under the comprehensive words *vasana* and *samskara*. These forces which form the core and motivation for human behaviour are not only the memory of the race but also that of the individual through his innumerable cycles of births. This collective memory of a person is not merely unconscious but guides his feelings and actions at all levels of psychic life. At birth he is formed of only these *vasanas* and *samskaras;* as he comes into contact with the environment, his ego slowly develops, with its various modes of affective activities at conscious strata—what is usually called emotional behaviour.

The word *rasa* is generally translated as emotion, relish, etc. A closer study would not warrant such a facile interpretation and hence it often is equated to 'aesthetic emotion'. However, it is best to omit the connotation of sentiment completely and translate it as 'aesthesis'. This distinction, though very fine, is yet a significant one.

Though *rasa* is itself not an excited state of mind, the emotional aspects of behaviour which go to form the substrate—though not the cause—of *rasa* have been analysed in great detail. It is not easy to find the modern Western psychological equivalents of these various factors which go to make an emotional state. For the points of view of the modern psychologist with a Western background and that of the ancient Indian psychologists are in many ways so different that such equations become incongruous. But garbing the ancient concepts in modern costumes makes for easier comprehension.

The factors that form the constituents of emotional action are, in Indian psychology, the following:

Vibhavas (the determinants): They are the causes of emotional responses. In modern terminology we may call them the stimulii or releasers. *Vibhavas* themselves are of two categories. *Alambana*—the person or object (or the idea of these) which acts as the stimulus. *Uddeepana*—the situation which is the context for such behaviour.

Anubhavas (the consequents): These form the responsive reactions. Obviously, with the Indian theory of emotion being closely linked to dramaturgy, this usually refers to overt expression.

Sattvabhavas (involuntary responses): They are also the bodily signs of emotion, in which are included both external and internal responses to *vibhavas*.

Bhavas: By this is meant the states of mind which are usually referred to as emotions. *Bhavas* are considered to be of two kinds (1) *sthayi bhavas* are the 'permanent' emotions and (2) *sanchari bhavas* are the transient moods. The essential difference between *sthayi* and *sanchari bhavas* seems to be that the former are more lasting and common to all human beings, and the latter more fleeting and characterized by the personal idiosyncracy of the individual. According to the generally accepted theories, there are nine differentia for the former and thirty seven for the latter.

Though *rasa* itself is identified with emotion, in most of the current literature, it is both emotional behaviour and more; *it is an awareness of the totality of the emotional situation.* It is a detached observance of such a condition of mind and body. This is a very important statement, the significance of which cannot be overemphasized.

"The experience of *rasa* is absolute and is known only by empathy. . . that is to say, by entering into, feeling the permanent motif". "Delightful or disgusting, exalted or lowly, obscure or refined, actual or imagery, there is no subject that cannot evoke *rasa* in man." While finally *rasa* is a contemplative state of mind, there are said to be nine *rasas* corresponding to nine emotional conditions: *sringara* (erotic), *hasya* (humorous), *karuna* (pathetic), *roudra* (furious), *veera* (valorous), *bhayanaka* (fearful), *beebhatsa* (odious), *adbhuta* (wonderous) and *santa* (peaceful).

Right from very ancient days attempts have been made to relate these specific *rasas* to music. Bharata said, for instance, that the ethos of a *jati* depended on the dominant note in it: *madhyama*–humorous, *panchama*-erotic, *shadja*-valorous, *rishabha*-furious, and so on. Sarangadeva (13th cent.) says that *shadja* and *rishaba* should be used for *veera* (valorous), *dhaivata* for *beebhatsa* (odious) and *bhayanaka* (fearful), *gandhara* and *nishada* for *karuna* (pathetic), *panchama* and *madhyama* for *hasya* (humorous).

In our own times, musicians have attributed moods to *ragas*. Melodies of *Khamaj* type, some say, are erotic, and those with *ma-dha* (F# -Ab) combinations express pathos and lassitude. Of course, there is not much doubt that the moods created do depend on the notes used and their interrelations, for the state of mind aroused by a set of consonant tones is surely different from that due to dissonant ones. But there is more to it. The highness or lowness of a tone, the nature of melodic movement (straight or meandering), the tempo and various other factors have their own part to play. Further, there is the often missed but vitally important element— *gamaka;* for such micro-variations and ornamentations of sounds contribute to a fullness and suppleness.

Very recently some experiments on current scientific lines were conducted by measuring the responses to defined phrases of a few *ragas*. It was found that they did produce fairly similar moods in all the listeners participating in the experiment, as instanced below:

Kafi: is very effective, humid, cool, soothing, light (not dense), deep; does not agitate.

Misra Mand: is pleasing, gay, refreshing, light, sweet; deep; does not agitate; has no feeling of novelty.

Pooriya Dhanasri: is sweet, colourful, deep, heavy, weary; reflects stability; cloudy; sacred; has no vitality.

Ragesri: is sweet, soothing, deep, weary, dark; no novelty and is inflexible; stable and calm.

In another set of studies, the relations of few *ragas* to their *rasas* were studied using present techniques in behavioural psychology, semantics, statistics and computerization. As an example: *raga Bhairav* of Hindustani music had *veera* (courageous), *bhayanaka* (fearful), *santa* (tranquil) and *rasas* (mental states). It was associated with autumn, early morning and white colour. These responses tally very well indeed with our ancient introspective descriptions of the *raga:* this is all the more significant as most of those who took part in the experiment were ignorant of our canonical music.

Closely linked with the ethos of a *raga* is its association with the seasons of the year and the time of the day, specially in Hindustani music. (South Indian music, however, has no such traditions, except for a small number of melodic types.) For example, the North Indian *Basant* and *Bahar* are of spring time. *Malhar* is of the rainy season; indeed, this *raga* is famous for its magical powers. It is believed that rains can be made to come down by singing it. Once the court musicians of Akbar became jealous of Tansen's eminence and friendship with the Emperor. To destroy him they played a ruse and suggested to Akbar that he command Tansen to sing *raga Deepak* (Melody of Lights), knowing fully well that it would burn him up. Not aware of such consequences, the Emperor requested the great singer to sing to him *Deepak*. The royal command could not be disobeyed; and so Tansen began to sing the *raga*. One by one the lamps in the palace courtyard, where he was performing, began to light up by themselves. As the music proceeded, the heat started to consume his body. The stupefied king did not know of a way to stop this slow but sure death. Then someone thought of Tansen's lady who was herself a great musician. She was immediately informed of the tragic situation. On hearing of the danger to her lover, she began to sing *raga Malhar* and surely the rains came, drenching Tansen and saving his life.

The seasonal association of *ragas* are grosser than diurnal relations. The immediate clues to this are the festivals of spring, rains, sowing and reaping. Of these, the most striking are the vernal and of monsoon with their sudden onset and deep biological symbols of procreation; they inspire music of the finest order, like the songs of *Vasant* (spring) and *Savan* (rains). *Raga Hindol* of the North is a good example. This is a *raga* invariably connected with the season of flowers and buds. *Hindola* "is a lovely youth surrounded by young ladies. He looks like an embodiment of love. The spring blossoms around him with all its beauty and lustre. He swings amongst maidens playing the *veenas* and beating the drums. Lord Brahma created him out of his navel-lotus." Now, the swing is one of the most ancient sexual auxiliary and symbol. It has always been recognized as an excitor of erotic desire and so the music sung with the swings (*dol*) was quite naturally named *Hindol*. In *raga* iconography, therefore, it is always represented by the swing. There are also similar associations of *Vasant* with spring and *Malhar* with rain.

The relation of *ragas* with diurnal variations is more definite; there is more order here. The musical qualities which determine the time of *raga* have not been satisfactorily examined, though Bhatkhande had attempted to find out some empirical rules of this psychological aspect. Earlier musicians and musicologists most often mention that such and such a *raga* is to be sung or played at such and such a time of the day or night. But few gave even an empirical analysis of this tradition. As a matter of fact, South Indian musicians do not recognize such restrictions at all, except for a couple of *ragas*. As found by Bhatkhande, the following generally determine the watch of the day for a *raga*:

1. *Tonal quality* : that is, whether the notes in the *raga* are *suddha* (natural), *komal* (flat) or *teevra* (sharp). Those with *ri, Ga, dha, Ni,* (Db, E, Ab, B) are twilight and dusk, when night and day pass into each other—a moment "pleased rather with some soft ideal scene, the work of fancy, or some happy tone of meditation, slipping in between the beauty coming and the beauty gone. . ." *Ragas* using *Ri, Ga, Dha, Ni,* (D, E, B, A) are of the first two watches of the day or night after twilight. During the third and the fourth watches of the day or night (12 noon—6 PM/12 midnight—6 AM) *ragas* with *ga* and *ni* (Eb, Bb) are sung.

2. *Tonal level* : by this is meant the position of a note in the octave. The octave is divided into two sections—*angas* (tetrachords). The lower tetrachord

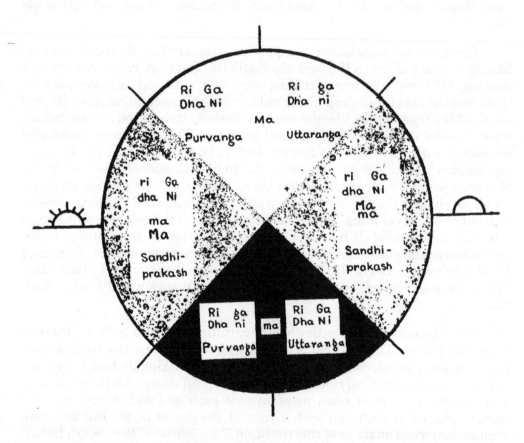

Fig 8.1 Raga–Time circle, Left: Sunrise, Right : Sunset. The eight watches of the day are shown by radial lines on the circumference 'Sandhiprakash is the time when day and night mingle, *vide* B.C. Deva, *Music of India; A Scientific Study.*

or *poorvanga* is from *Sa* to *Pa* (C to G); the upper section, *uttaranga,* extends from *Ma* to Sa¹ (F to C¹). This is shown thus :

Sa	ri	Ri	ga	Ga	Ma	ma	Pa	dha	Dha	ni	Ni	Sa¹
C	Db	D	Eb	E	F	F#	G	Ab	A	Bb	B	C¹

Poorvanga

Uttaranga

If a *raga* has a *vadi* in the lower section, it is called a *poorva raga;* if, on the other hand, the *vadi* is in the upper tetrachord, it is an *uttara raga.* The convention is that *poorva ragas* are to be performed between midday and midnight; *uttara ragas* are to limited to the period from midnight to midday.

Of great significance in all this is *teevra madhyama* (F sharp). The introduction of this note again indicates the passing of twilight *ragas* into the later ones. As Venkatamakhi, an author of the 17th century remarks, "Just by a drop of curd, a jar of sweet milk is changed into curd; so by the addition of *ma,* a *poorva raga* is changed into an *uttara raga.*" (See Figure 8.1).

How far is this classification of *ragas* with respect to time scientific? In other words, is it only a fanciful habit of tradition or is it possible to experimentally establish such temporal associations? First is the fact that the South Indian system does not accept such an elaborate and fairly rigid arrangement. Indeed, except for a few *ragas,* there is no restriction of time at all. This only means that the hypothesis of *raga*-time does not apply to the whole of Indian music. Secondly, there has been no systematic investigation into this very interesting psychological aspect of *raga.* Till we do have properly established results, we can at present take all this as traditional conditioning. Thirdly, how does one reconcile patterns of mixed *ragas,* when such an admixture is of those melodies of different times of the day? As an instance, there is a *raga* called *Bhairav-Bahar;* this is a combination of *Bhairav* (early hours of the morning) and *Bahar* (late night). Now what could be the time for such a fused *raga?*

In any case, such a confinement of *ragas* to time and season is now slackening. The necessities of scheduling public concerts, the limitations of radio broadcasting and the change in the modes of life due to urbanization are all slowly altering these and other musical attitudes, loosening the traditional rules.

Indian art, whether it be painting, poetry, dance or music has a characteristically inward quality. This is a manifestation of the bias and world-view of this culture. The nature of creation and its forces are not felt and thought about commencing at the point of material phenomena. "Indian thought at its deepest affirms, on the other hand, that mind and matter are rather different grades of the same energy, different organizations of one conscious Force of Existence". Hence the external and its imitation have had little place in our art. The outside is only a projection of this "Force of Existence", experienced within and "beauty does not arise from the subject of a work of art, but from the necessity that has been felt of representing that subject." That is why programmatic music is not considered of really deep quality and it is a recent occurrence in the country, specially with the ballet and the films. Imitation of thunder and the ripple of water is not great music, just as realistic photographic painting is not great art. The languor of rains after an Indian summer is what *Malhar* expresses but not the patter of drops on a tin-roof!

A *raga* or a *tala* is, therefore, the externalization of an inner consciousness. It is a concept or a mood unfolding itself. This 'concept' has also been iconized. For every *raga* is a man, a woman or a god in a particular state of mind. In effect, it is a personality—a *dhyanamoorty*—a form to be meditated upon and the *dhyanamoorty* helps and intensifies the inward tendency of the artiste. "Let the imager establish images in temples by meditation on the deities who are the object of his devotion. . . In no other way, not even by direct and immediate vision of an actual object, is it possible to be so absorbed in contemplation."

Narada, the divine singer, was boastful of his musical genius; and Lord Vishnu wanted to teach him a lesson in humility. So the Lord invited the sage for a walk in the woods. As they were going along, they heard wails and moans, coming from a nearby cave. Their curiosity and pity aroused, the two entered the place and found men and women—all maimed—weeping and writhing in pain. Lord Vishnu solicitously enquired as to the cause of their sorrow. Amid their sobs they said, "O Lord, how shall we describe our agony. We are the *dhyanamoortys* of *ragas* and *raginis*. There is a churl called Narada who thinks he is a great musician but does not know a thing. See how he has sung everything wrongly and broken our arms and legs and disfigured our faces!" It was a sufficient lesson to Narada and to all musicians; it is not easy to grasp the essential form of a *raga* and to project it without confusion.

This iconography of *ragas* has produced for us the exquisite *raga-mala* miniatures of North India. The six major *ragas,* their wives, sons and daughters-in-law have all been given more or less definite situations of emotion and are depicted in such states. *Ragini Todi* is the beautiful maiden with a *veena* on her shoulders and enchanted deer as her company; the ascetic and the snakes always portray the mood of *ragini Asavari.*

A *raga* or *ragini,* thus, is a hero or a heroine in a given emotional condition and a musician is expected to create this effective state and the audience to participate in this creation. That is why a listener, of really fine sensitivity, is a *rasika* and *sahridaya-*a person who can attain to a state of *rasa* and one who attains the condition of empathy.

Of course, not all music is 'contemplative' of the Force of Existence. The sensate value in human experience is not taboo in good art, and they find expression in the lyrical songs of *thumri, tappa,* and *javali.* These are certainly of an earthly quality like the sculpture of Konarak. It is how one creates music or responds to it that matters.

An actual performance or concert is not always or constantly a piece of high art. As Indian music is mainly improvisational, moments of great creation are rare. But then, improvization is not the correct word, for there is no total extemporization. The *raga* and *tala* have been studied and practised thoroughly before coming on to the concert platform. Even certain phrases and idioms are preset. But in the main, it is an expression of the mood of the *raga* and *tala* as the performer understands it at the moment. This mood is unitary; there are no clashes nor opposites. However, the finer fringes and overtones of the *bhava* are presented by means of delicate *gamakas,* change in tempo and rhythm. The unexpected constantly rides over the expected. It is a virtuoso approach: it is not *what* is done that is important but *how* well it is done.

9

Then and Now

THE STRIKING CHARACTERISTIC of Indian society is both its variegated strains of influence as well as its partial isolation from outside incursions, sometimes for centuries. The great age of this subcontinent itself presents serious problems in the historicity of cultural dynamics. The geographical spread of the land poses questions of social exchanges of unbelievable complexity.

In any cultural study of this country, the parts played by various races and tribes are the most important and can never be forgotten. As a matter of fact, it is the understanding of the contribution of these that can give us a clear picture of the changing horizons of Indian music. For, the present concept of *raga* is but often a highly sophisticated form grown from an archiac folk or tribal tune; what is now an intricate instrument like *veena* is but a refined *Kinnari*.

The present society of India, then, is a resultant of the interaction of races and cultures, indigenous and foreign. The Negrito, the Mongoloid, the Dravidian and the Aryan have all contributed to this active agglomerate. Their part in the development of our music can be observed in the names of many *ragas*; for instance, tribal adjectives like *chenchu, yerukalu* to melodies are proof of such possible origins. Names like *Malava, Gurjari, Karnata* and so on indicate regional associations.

While these musical elements are some of the bases, religious music is another direction of influence. So far the only ecclesiastical chant of antiquity of which we have sound knowledge is the Vedic. From single and double notes, it grew into a simple one of three notes — the lower grave (*anudatta*), the higher accented (*udatta*) and the middle (*svarita*). This gradually evolved into a heptatonic scale of *Samaveda,* the recitation of which was descending one with a scale resembling roughly the Greek Phrygic mode (the scale of D) and the current *Bagesri raga* of North India. Obviously this was an Aryan psalmody and greatly influenced all later codifications.

During the period after the Vedic chants, we come across what is known as the *gandharva* and *margi sangeeta*. This was also a kind of sacred music, Lord Siva being the subject. Even prior to these were, perhaps, the ballads based on the epics of *Ramayana* and *Mahabharata,* sung to the accompaniment of *veena* (harp) and flute. The best known episode of this epoch was the recitation of *Ramayana* by Lava and Kusa, the sons of Rama. They were trained by immortal Valmiki who sent them to the court of Rama to sing his own tale, telling them, "If King Rama invites you to sing, you should perform before the sages gathered there according to the manner taught by me. . . Do not aspire for money, for it has no value for a hermit living on fruit and roots. . ."

What was this music like? Obviously, it is impossible to reconstruct it, but this much is known: There were two standard scales called *gramas*. The melodic types were known as *jatis* and these in turn were based on *moorcchanas,* which were derived scales from *gramas*. The *jatis* were differentiated from one another in their tonics or key-notes, notes of commencement and stasis, etc. The most significant work of this period, Bharata's *Natyasastra* (2nd cent. A.D.), gives detailed descriptions of the musical art of that age of Indian history, as it deals with such aspects like *sruti, grama,* instruments and so on.

However, the concept of *raga* takes a definite shape by the time of Matanga (5th cent. A.D.). In his *Brihaddesi* he describes what was then called *desi sangeeta,* the secular or profane music — hence the name of the book (*brihat* = great, *desi* = regional, secular). The treatise deals with *desi ragas* which were contradistinct to the *Marga ragas*. While the latter were ecclesiastical in purport, the former varied from region to region and were for "pleasing the minds of men". As the texts say, "That music, source of all growth, seen in the beginning by the Creator in His Contemplation, performed by Bharata and other sages in the presence of resplendent Siva, is the music of contemplation (*marga* - the path)", whereas, "the song, dance and play of instruments, different from country to country and performed as their people please, and which charms the heart are called *desi* (secular)".

A monumental work came to be written in the 13th cent. A.D. This was the *Sangeeta Ratnakara* (The Ocean of Music) penned by Sarangadeva, an emigrant from Kashmir, who became the Chief Accountant of Raja Sodhala, a Yadava king of Devgiri in South India. :A work so stupendous in depth and extent it is, that it is difficult to believe it could have been scribed by one man. The *Ratnakara* gives in great detail descriptions of scales, *ragas*, *talas*, musical forms, instruments and many other subjects. Of greater significance is the fact that it is, perhaps, the first major work dealing with Northern and Southern musical systems. It is opined by many scholars, though we need not discuss the validity of this opinion here, that it was during this period that Indian music got bifurcated into the two systems of North and South.

Of the other important tributary, the Dravidian, we do not have any information before the 2nd cent. A.D. The Indus Valley civilization, which is supposed to be pre-Vedic and Dravidian, does not offer any clue in its remains. Excavations have brought to light, so far, only a clay whistle. But from the 2nd to about the 6th century A.D. we come across in Tamil classics, like the *Silappadikaram,* descriptions of a highly developed system. Details of melodic schemes called *panns* and intervals known as *alagu* are given.

By about the 15th century a certain degree of uniformity in Indian music seems to have been achieved. By then the concept of *grama, moorcchana* and *jati* is completely superceded by *raga,* one standard scale and a twelve-tone arrangement of notes within the gamut. It is this new frame which forms the base of today's music.

There is a gradual interaction of the various types and today we have two broadly similar systems of music—Hindustani (North Indian) and Carnatic (South Indian). The two are so similar in fundamentals that they are considered as dialectal differences of 'one' musical language. Essentially both are melodic; and they follow more or less the same rules of *raga* construction. The concept of *tala* is also common to both. However, there are differences which make these two quite distinct complexes. With greater facilities of communication, a fast exchange of techniques and ideas is taking place, the differences are reduced in course of time.

As for musical forms, the main one before *dhrupad* was *prabandha,* the word itself having a general connotation, 'closed form'. More specifically, it meant a kind of composition with four sections. Of such a type was Jayadeva's *Geeta Govinda* (13th cent.), an operatic poem of twelve cantos, written in Sanskrit. Yet to be rivalled in quality, it is also the first musical work that we know of which gives both the *raga* and *tala* for every one of its songs. The *prabandha* period is followed by the age of *dhrupad* which reached its height of popularity by about the 16th to 17th centuries. With the decline in the appeal of *dhurpad, kheyal* took the prime place and to this day is the most respected and accepted concert form in North India. In the South, *tevarams* of the Tamil land are the most ancient sophisticated music which we have definite information about. These were the sacred hymns composed by the three saints — Tirujnana Sambandar, Appar and Sundaramoorty Nayanar (7th-9th cent.). The *Tiruppukazh,* another bunch of devotional songs were the creation of a Saivaite saint. *Tevarams* have only their *panns* (melodic schemes) mentioned but not their *talas,* in the case of *Tiruppukazh* only their *talas* are given, not their melodic titles. (Hence the significance of the *Geeta Govinda* wherein the names of *ragas* and *talas* for all *prabandhas* are clearly shown.) The next major form is *keertana.* Earliest composers of this kind of musical schemata were the Tallapakkam poets (15th cent). The texts of their songs were inscribed on copper plates, preserved to this day in the archives of the temple in Tirupati. This musical type gets a great fillip at the hands of Purandaradasa and is chiselled to its finest by the *Trimoorty*: Tyagaraja, Syama Sastry and Muthuswami Dikshitar.

Pari Passu with all this a great change came over the structure and style of playing of musical instruments. Vedic *veenas* were of the harp, lyre and dulcimer types. We hear of *vipanchi* (nine stringed) and *sata tantri* (hundred stringed) *veenas;* some of these, along with *venu* (flute) were used for Vedic chant. Perhaps, due to the excessive influence of vocal music with its glides, shakes and trills such instruments were found inadequate. Or else, there were deeper psychological reasons. In any case, these harps and dulcimers disappeared completely by about the 15th cent., giving place to fingerboard instruments. Today we have *sitar, sarod* and *veena* (fingerboard lutes) as the most popular and accepted ones. The stray survivors of the ancient *veenas* are *santoor* and *svaramandal.*

One of the major imports from outside India was the music of Central Asia, Persia and Arabia. Influence of Arabic music can be seen even now in the songs and tunes of the Indian islands of the Arabian Sea. A *raga* like *Hijaj* points to its Arabic origin, Hijaj being an area in Arabia. *Raga Turushka Todi* obviously is indicative of its Central Asian source. More than anything else, these incursions have affected the style of singing, particularly in North India. For instance, *ghazals* (love lyrics), *tappas* and music of that genre are definitely foreign. These Central and West Asian cultures have also given to India bowed instruments like *sarangi* and perhaps even some long-necked lutes.

A key figure in the spread of Muslim—or rather Persian—musical feelings and technique was Amir Khusro (1254-1324 A.D.), though even prior to him the effects of invasions from Central and Western Asia were felt; for in 1013 A.D., Mohammad Gaznavi plundered North-West India disturbing a settled culture. Many an artiste and scholar fled Kashmir and neighbouring areas seeking asylum in the South, the most famous of them being Sarangadeva, the author of *Sangeeta Ratnakara* (13th century). With them they carried their art and scholarship which they would not divulge to *mlecchas* (alien barbarians). So a state of confusion prevailed, with a wide gulf between the more ancient grammar and the then current practice.

It was in this atmosphere that Amir Khusro lived. He was a mentor and adviser to eleven rulers of Delhi, particularly of the Khilji dynasty, and, being an astute politician, kept his head on his shoulders when many were falling. He was also a Sufi and loved poetry and music. While a scholar in Persian, he had also learnt Brij Bhasa and Sanskrit, perhaps, because his mother was a Hindu and father a Muslim. Khusro composed *qauls* and *taranas,* and wrote in Persian and Brij. More than anything, he attempted to 'synthesise' Persian music and Indian music which he learned. The origin of *kheyal* and the invention of *sitar* are attributed to him, though he himself does not mention this fact. But his personality does seem to have influenced both politics and art both in his time and later on.

A few centuries (primarily after the 13th cent.) of Muslim invasion and rule, which extended even to South India, brought in their wake a changed perspective. Because Islam does not permit music as a part of its ritual, it was necessarily fostered outside the place of worship. Hence, an element of physical pleasure, particularly of the courtier, became predominant. What was perhaps closely associated with both temples and royal courts in earlier times came to confined to only the courts and their kingly pleasures. This is not to deny any religious music of the Muslims; a notable trend was that of Sufism which did affect considerably the content of compositions made by Muslim musicians. No doubt the older music still survived in Hindu temples and rites. But Hindu philosophy had become so highly esoteric that the common man in his busy life had neither the time nor the energy to follow the complicated theological texts and commentaries. As a reaction to both these—the fast growing alien influences and withdrawal of Hindu religion from the personal intimacy of daily life-came the *bhakti* (adoration) movement. This flood of emotional devotion threw up great composers and musicians. Music came to the people as devotional songs and spread from home to home.

Much has been written about what is known as the *bhakti* movement in India. While there was definitely an upsurge of devotional element in Indian life in medieval times, it would be wrong to limit such feelings to any part of human history. The devotion to something superhuman is as old, perhaps, as man. From primitive magic and totem worship to the greatest mystic it is in one direction: the beseeching of Grace.

Historically speaking, the Vedic hymns to Varuna, Savitri and Ushas may be some of the earliest songs and rhapsodies of prayer; however, the best known devotional songs are connected with the Vaishnavaite movement in South India. But even prior to this, the Saivaite psalms had seeped in the culture of this land. The hymnody of Manikkavachakar called *Tiruvachakam* and *Tevarams* of Appar, Sambandar and Sundaramoorthy (known as *Nayanars)* are some of the finest lyrics devoted to Siva. Similarly the *vachanas* of *Veera Saivas* of Karnatak have inspired millions. The revered *Veera Saiva* saintly minister, Basava, calls out, "Like the cow lost in the jungle, I cry, Amba! Amba! I shall be calling, God Koodala Sangama, till You tell me, 'Live thou and be immortal'".

Following these was the all-embracing *bhakti* current starting with the Vaishnavaite Alvars of Tamil land. They decried social bifurcations and injustice, and sang of devotion and surrender. Ramanuja (12th-13th cent.), a gem of the brightest hue in this garland, was a profound personality and gave a new turn to religious life. His teachings started the initial ripples of a wave of *bhakti* throughout India. While Sankara's thought-experiences are some of the greatest in the world, they demanded an uncompromising understanding of the One-a state of mind too dizzy for appeal. Vaishnavaite think-feeling makes the Godhead a personal being, almost anthropomorphic. One could love, abuse, play or quarrel with such a God! Hence the intense emotional attraction of Ramanuja and Madhva, the latter to even greater degrees. For *bhakti* or devotion becomes the closest attachment of the Mind of Man to the Godhead.

The influence of Madhva (13th cent. A.D) deserves further mention. His Order produced not only eminent philosophers like Vyasaraya, but also a whole lineage of *Haridasas*—Servants of God—who carried the message of love and devotion from door to door through their soul-stirring songs. Among these was the greatest of the great, Sri Purandaradasa. He was not only a saint of the highest mystic experience and *bhakti* but also a pioneering musician, and has come to be known as the Father of Carnatic Music.

The wave of *bhakti* spread from South India and engulfed the whole of the subcontinent. Mainly because of Ramananda (14th cent), it became an irresistible force in the religious and musical life of the North. The movement pulled down caste barriers and religious obscurantism, and gave us some of the most brilliant mystic singers of North India. Kabir, Dadu, Namdev, Tukaram, Nanak, Chaitanya, Meera and a host of others who poured forth *bhajans* and *abhangas* which have become an integral part of Indian musical and religious life. The tide took in its stride the Sufis of Islam.

A stream of this flow created the Radha-Krishna love legends which have become the source of inspiration for some of the most beautiful songs. The incomparable *Geeta Govinda* of Jayadeva, the *keertans* of Chaitanya and the *padams* of Kshetrayya have sublimated the human man-woman love to the finest gossamer Mystic Adoration.

While earlier devotional music was mostly hymnic or folk-melodic, a few composers like Jayadeva, Purandaradasa. Bhadrachala Ramdas created music and poetry of high excellence. Then came Tyagaraja about two hundred years ago. His music was divine both in form and content. He decried social pretences and self-aggrandizement in the name of *yoga*. He says, "To the great one who has control over his mind, where is the need for *tantra* and *mantra*". Again, *"Rama nama* is the precious thing to be coveted. Why bother with other paths?" And what should one's singing be like? "Devotion with the nectar of note and melody is verily a paradise. One attains salvation when one becomes a *jnani* (an intelligent knower), after several births; but he who has the knowledge of *raga* sung with natural devotion is a liberated soul."

In our own times the music of Rabindranath Tagore has once again raised music to high pinnacles of meditative grandeur. For him all creation is music, "The light of thy music illumines the world. The life-breath of thy music runs from sky to sky."

Sri Aurobindo is supposed to have remarked somewhere that there is not an inch of India where a saint has not walked. One may be permitted to add that there is not an inch of India where a *bhakta* has not walked and sung.

The end of the Muslim period brings us to the doorstep of the contemporary scene. As we survey this panorama, once again it becomes evident that the change Indian music is undergoing is again one of style and presentation and not of its foundation. For, the music is still essentially melodic, though foreign colourings are slowly but inevitably creeping in.

There is an important factor which has given a new impetus to Indian life: the struggle for and attainment of political freedom. During the twenties it was a patriotic fervor that drew many musicians into the whirlpool of nationalistic struggle and those included Rabindranath Tagore, D.L. Roy, Kazi Nazrul Islam of Bengal, Vishnu Digamber Paluskar of Maharashtra, Bharati the Tamil poet and others, with an urge to establish our music and musicology on the world map, pulling it out of the quagmire of neglect by the English educated 'elite'. There were also institutions which took up the challenge of the renaissance—such as the Theosophical Society, the Madras Music Academy, the Visva Bharati University to mention the foremost. And strangely enough this resurgence was helped by foreign scholars like Willard, Jones, Strangways, Popley, Cousins and others. After the forties, schools were encouraged to have classes in music and State governments also started conducting examinations. On the profit side, it meant a spread of musical interest and the increase in employment potential of music teachers; on the loss side, it has meant a regrettable lowering of standards and tastes as well as a proliferation of 'tution classes' and 'guide books'.

Contemporary music has been deeply affected by contact with Western industrial civilization and scientific thinking. This is seen not only in the practice of the art but in musical life in general too; also in its evaluation as entertainment, preservation, research in folk music, education and so on.

The new directions are too near in time to be assessed as progressive or otherwise. But it is possible, at least, to describe them as far as contemporary objectivity permits. Once again, the change in the horizon of Indian music is not in the basic technique but in the social attitude towards music. Fundamentally the music is still one of *raga* and *tala,* but there is a dynamic alteration in style and point of view.

The most significant outcome of this cultural interaction is in the change-over from a feudal to a managerial society. A feudal society is more or less governed by an individual; but in the present set-up it is a group that is responsible for the management of social order. In the process of change, individual-to-individual communication has lost its meaning and individual-to-mass contact has become the directing force.

Till about a generation ago, the royal court or the petty feudal lord was the patron of music. The artiste maintained by him was assured of a source of secure living and had any length of time to study and practise; and the royal audience had any amount of leisure to listen. Religious endowments and temples, the other major patrons of music, were not inclined to hurry. On the contrary, they insisted on gravity and profundity. The music was, therefore, leisurely with an intense (often even exaggerated) individuality. The economic situation was also less competitive than now and a musician could take things slower. But it would not be right to assume that all was wonderfully healthy, for much must have depended on the idiosyncracy of the patron and the sycophancy of the courtiers.

This class of art-lovers has been replaced by the concert-goers: mostly middle class businessmen, professionals and office managers. They have no time to take a music performance leisurely, for their lives are keyed to faster tempos. Since they pay less fees individually, mass audience has become common and necessary to support a musician. Because princely houses can now no more afford such expenditure, they have also lost their status symbol. Even the temples, with their dwindled coffers, are not in a position to maintain artists. So it has become now the responsibility of the people in general and the new government of the people in particular to further the interests of the arts.

As a governmental agency the All India Radio is the biggest patron of music. With its large and ramifying network it has been able to draw upon extensive talent. Local artistes, who would otherwise have no large audience, go on the air and can be listened to by a much greater population than a few years ago. However, since the AIR has to meet the demands of the public in general, it cannot afford to be always highbrow. Some years ago there was a controversy over the starting of the *Vividh Bharati* broadcast which was directed towards those who wanted 'lighter' entertainment rather than the 'heavier' classical music. But the wish of the populace prevailed. The next logical step was since taken with the introduction of the commercial services of the AIR.

Another big step which the Government took was the establishment of the Sangeet Natak Akademies. This was, indeed, a step in the right direction, for the Government had to have organizations that could look after and foster the arts on the academic side. So, we now have an Akademi in almost every State and one at the Centre. The very establishment of such bodies was an encouraging sign, an evidence of purposeful thinking. Some of the Akademies have done good work. Archives of music and dance—records and films—have been built up. Libraries have been made available for reference and research. A few publications brought out show signs of some activity. Seminars are held and programmes presented. The Akademies also bestow Awards and Fellowships to eminent personalities in the field of music, dance and drama.

The effects of all these newer trends have been striking. Radio broadcasting and gramaphone have also had singular influence, for the technical limitations have affected the musical style, mainly due to the restrictions of programming. The two main forces—mass audience and technological communicative media—have produced certain changes worth noting.

First is the loss of personal rapport between the artiste and the listeners. A huge audience can never have a personal appeal to the musician. The radio listener and the disc purchaser are not even physically and mentally present for the artiste. He is not therefore, in a position to know the immediate response of the listener, which is an integral part of Indian musical feeling which relies so much on the immediacy of creative inspiration, eliciting an immediate appreciation. As a result of this, Indian music is losing the intimacy of personal communication.

Secondly, there has been an abridgement of psyche. The urban audience and broadcasting programmes cannot afford to have long expositions. Hence, the old *mehfils* (soirees) have virtually ceased to exist, being replaced by big indifferent audiences fed by the public address system. Since the audiences are mostly conditioned by short-lived habits, the present day music has developed idioms of short phrases and quick movements. A rapidity of feeling and a compression of mood is gaining ground; all this of course, does not mean that music has lost quality: only the idiom has changed.

As against these, there have been salutary consequences. The most important is the availability of music of the highest order to everyone. One need not be a courtier to have an opportunity of listening to chamber music; one can, without heavy expense, go to public concerts, listen to the radio or disc. This is building an unprecedented social awareness to art. This awareness it is true, is not always discriminative, but is a compelling force on the artist to express himself effectively.

Another outcome is on the life of the musician himself. Till within recent memory, he was generally outside social currents and was not 'respectable'. He, on the contrary, lived aloof and kept his virtuosity as a 'trade secret'. With changed conditions, he has had to come out and teach without reservations and live in a quick and competitive world. His 'ivory tower' is crumbling. Also, the musician is no more unhonoured; on the contrary, artistes are now being bestowed with some of the highest honours of the State.

The social attitude to music has also had another profound repercussion and that is in the field of musical education. The traditional method was known as the *gurukula vasa*; an apprenticeship, living with the *guru* (preceptor). The disciple stayed with the *guru* and served him. The *guru* in his turn looked after the student and taught him the art. There was no regular syllabus or examinations. It was a patient, hard and intensive training. But the method was very effective, for the tutelage left nothing to chance and there was no hurry to 'complete the course'.

This way of musical training is slowly going out of vogue. Advanced students still go to a *guru;* but the training is more in the form of paid tuitions than as the old way of living with the teacher and absorbing his art. Normal training in music is now mostly institutionalized. Schools, colleges and universities offer courses in music, there are also professional institutions which prescribe syllabi of study and examinations. This system has enabled a larger public to learn music thus taking the art to even humble homes. But while such a method is extensive, it is not intensive. Teaching students in groups, prescription of rigid syllabus, conducting 'examinations'—all these have reduced the depth of understanding. The products of such pedagogy rarely become good artistes or teachers. The impasse is now agitating those responsible for the training of students and attempts at finding a creative synthesis of the old and the new are being made.

Western influence has been particularly felt in the orchestration of our music. India in ancient times did know of instrumental ensembles. They were called *kutapa. Kutapas* of various types were used in dramas for emotional effects. But harmonization in the Western sense was unknown and it is even alien to the spirit and technique of Indian music. However, contact with West has now brought orchestras. Princely houses used to maintain Western bands and the Armed Forces have also such orchestras-some of them as imitative remnants of the British. Even schools parade small ensembles. Brass bands playing out of context tunes from films are a 'must' in marriages. The All India Radio, a Governmental organization, has a full-fledged orchestra, called the *Vadya Vrinda,* which has tried to 'harmonize' *ragas.* However, the most obvious effective impact of orchestration and harmony has been in film music. Musicians there have not been fettered by tradition; and their purpose is to entertain and produce programmatic effect. For this they have borrowed freely from the West, as what Indian music lacks in volume and tone-colour is provided by such expediency. Even the approach has veered to jazz, rock'n roll and pop music, as they are very catchy and exciting — and this is what fetches box-office returns.

An interesting phenomenon is the pull from the West. Ruled and dominated by the West for some centuries, most Indians still have an attraction to Europe and America. This is both psychological and, of course, financial. With the enormously growing interest there in Indian music, our country has started exporting musical instruments and *yoga,* along with musicians and *yogis* of various degrees of qualities and integrities. Some of our best known artistes are more famous abroad than here, and certainly better paid, and they condescend to visit us once in a while, playing what they have not yet lost! The effect on their music is palpable; and being divorced from their psychic sustenance here, the music they dish out has become superficial, has lost its Indian idiom and acquired a big dash of inanity.

Yet another trend that is invading and may change the dimensions of our music is the East-West encounter. We have just noted the effects of Indian musicians going West and absorbing new idioms. But perhaps what may be more effective is the modern Western composers invading India and producing 'harmonized' *ragas.* They have started 'composing' in *ragas*: with knowledge of varying depths. True, sometimes such music by itself is beautiful. But it robs the *raga* of almost all its essentials like microtonal differentia, (for often tempered instruments are used and trans-positions indulged in), essential *gamakas,* characteristic *chalan* or *sanchar* and above all an inwardness and a feeling of growth which is our genius. Who knows not what pernicious effects these new directions may have. The *avant- garde* may call any reaction to this as 'purist'. But then, it is certainly better to be pure than to be foolish and exhibit ignorance as 'creativity'.

Whether all these impacts-technical and social-will eventually change the entire form of and attitude to music in India, no one can predict. It can only be hoped that it will not lose its meditative inward quality and delicateness of structure.

10

Among the Great

TYAGARAJA SANG in humility, "Many are the great souls; to them all my salutations". In its long and chequered history, music has received new impetus and orientation—in its form, style and or content. These have been given fresh life and have even turned the tide of social appreciation, because of the men and women who were behind such movements. No account of our music can be complete without a study of their lives and contributions.

Jayadeva

"If thy spirit seeks to brood
On Hari glorious, Hari good;
If it feeds on solemn numbers,
Dim as dreams and soft as slumbers,
Lend thine ear to Jayadeva,
Lord of all the spells that save".

So wrote Jayadeva, the immortal, whose Sanskrit poem, *Geeta Govinda,* is one of the greatest landmarks in the history of Indian music. Of the musical influences that have shown new paths to our culture, it should be ranked with the *Devaranamas* of Purandaradasa, the *kritis* of Tyagaraja, *dhrupads* of Swami Haridas and the *kheyals* of Sadarang and Adrang. All of them have either given us new forms or created music of the highest quality in a pre-existing style. *Geeta Govinda* is, however, unique in many ways. Undoubtedly, it is a magnificent musical composition; but even as literature it has almost no equals. Apart from the beauty of language, its content is of the finest mystic adoration. *Geeta Govinda* has been also used as an excellent theme for dance. Great paintings have been inspired by it.

Jayadeva Goswami, the author of *Geeta Govinda,* lived in the 12th-13th century. There is some doubt regarding the place of his birth. It is believed that he was born in Kendubilva, a small hamlet in the Birbhum district of

Bengal. Some are, however, of the opinion that his birth place was Bindubilva in Orissa. Not much is known of his ancestry either. Some claim that his fore-fathers came from Punjab and some say Gujarat. Jayadeva's father was Bhojadeva and his mother Radha Devi (Rama Devi, Vama Devi). Padmavati was his wife. There is a story of Jayadeva's marriage to her. Jayadeva was left an orphan even when he was a child. He does not seem to have had any worldly desires or ambitions and took to wandering like a mendicant with the name of Hari on his lips. Eventually he reached Puri in Orissa. There a Brahmin, Sudeva, had a daughter, his first born, Padmavati He had vowed to give his first child to Lord Jagannath. Adhering to his vow he wanted to hand over the girl to the Lord's temple. But Sudeva was told in a dream that he should hand her in marriage to the pilgrim Jayadeva. Perhaps the poor mendicant did protest about his utter incapability to support a wife. But Padmavati was married to the hapless fellow, as it was Lord Jagannath's command. Though poor in wordly goods then, the couple lived an extremely happy life.

Jayadeva was recognized in his own times as a very great poet. He was received with honour and made the court poct by Raja Laksmana Sena of Nabadweep, Bengal. The King (1178-1205 A.D.) was the son of Vallala Sena, himself a great scholar. This family of Sena rulers were most probably from South India, as they called themselves as *Karnata Kshatriyas*.

The text of *Geeta Govinda* deals with the Radha-Krishna theme:

> *"Thy sky is clouded; and the wood resembles*
> *The sky, thick- arched with black Tamala boughs;*
> *O Radha, Radha! take this Soul, that trembles*
> *In life's deep midnight, to thy golden house.*
> *So Nanda spoke—and, led by Radha's spirit*
> *The feet of Krishna found the road aright*
> *Wherefore, in bliss which all high hearts inherit,*
> *Together taste they Love's divine delight."*

The work contains twelve chapters, comprising twenty-four *astapadis* (songs) interspersed with *slokas* (verses). The subject of the poems is typically of *Vaishnavaite* devotion: the separation of Radha (devotee) from the Adored (Krishna) due to Ignorance (jealousy, self-importance and so on). The *guru (sakhi)* dispels the ignorance of Radha, invokes the blessings of the Lord and brings about the Union of the two. The Godhead Himself suffers pangs of separation from the devotee and it is due to His infinite patience and Grace that the devotee surrenders finally to the Will of the Lord.

This mystical experience is allegorised by Jayadeva in his work through erotic symbolism. His descriptions are very realistic but at once deeply moving and beautiful. There is not a single word of pornographic intent. The mutual love of Radha and Krishna is intense but delicate – *madhura bhakti,* the essence of *Vaishnavaite* adoration.

We do not have any knowledge of how exactly the *astapadis* were rendered. In construction they are songs usually with eight sections or *padas;* that is why they are called *astapadis (asta* eight, *pada* feet, line). They were composed as *prabandhas* which were a type of closed forms in known *ragas* and *talas.* Though Jayadeva mentions the *raga* and *tala* for each *astapadi,* the original mode of singing is lost to us. With its migration to various parts of the country, the work has acquired new music, according to the prevalent local style. The famous Indologist, Sir William Jones said, "When I first read the songs of Jayadeva, who has prefaced to each the name of the mode in which it was to be sung, I had hopes of procuring the original music; but the Pandits of the South referred me to those of the West, and the Brahmans of the West would have sent me to those of the North, while those of Nepal and Kashmir declared that they had no ancient music, but imagined that the notes of the *'Geeta Govinda'* must exist, if anywhere, where the poet was born". There are traditional styles of more or less antiquity in every region of the country. For example, Maharana Kumbha of Mewar (15th cent.) gave his own music to the songs. In Tamil Nadu, Ramudu Bhagavatar (17th cent.) set the *astapadis* to music in Carnatic style. There are other local musical varieties, including the *Granth Sahib,* or the 'Bible' of the Sikhs. Modern singers of *dhrupads* and *kheyals* also have adapted the lyrics to suit their needs. And the greatness of the language and prosody of *Geeta Govinda* is such that it has lent itself to all these styles. It has inspired similar works like the *Sivastapadi* of Chandrasekhara Sarasvati, the *Ramastapadi* by Rama Kavi. Some people even surmise that Tyagaraja modelled his opera, *Nouka Charitram,* on *Geeta Govinda.*

That o expressive song-poems should have been danced to is but natural. Perhaps his wife, Padmavati, herself danced to his music; for he writes of himself as one who guides the dancing feet of Padmavati. We know for certain that *Geeta Govinda* is almost indispensablein Odissi dance, as by a royal decree Prataparudra Deva of Puri (15 cent.) made it compulsory that only these songs should be sung in the temple of Lord Jagannatha. It is quite probable that the theme and text travelled from Orissa to Andhra influencing the Kuchipudi dance and it seems to have been a part of the repertoire of some Bharatanatyam dancers as well. *Geeta Govinda* has also evidently had an impact on the dance of Kerala; for Krishnanattam, the text of which is a close imitation of this work, gradually flowered into Kathakali which uses *astapadis* from *Geeta Govinda* in its preliminary portions.

They say that a "picture is a voiceless poem, a poem a vocal picture." The extraordinary beautiful feeling of these songs has been visualized by our painters. The story of the love of Radha and Krishna is painted so delicately and daintily that they might have been done by Jayadeva himself, if he had been a painter. With the spreading of Vaishnavism and its *bhakti,* the Radha-Krishna lore became a favourite of painters in the western and northern parts of India; what greater poem could there be to illustrate than this? We get the early Gujarat pictures, a series from Jaunpur and even in Mohgul style. Rajasthan has given us miniatures done under the commission of Rajas Sangram Singh and Kalyan Singh. The magnificent "voiceless poems" of Kangra and Basohli testify to the undying source of creation that is *Geeta Govinda*.

Swami Haridas

Swami Haridas has a highly significant place in the music of North India, for the era in which he lived was an extremely active and productive one. Therefore, Haridas found a fecund environment to give of his best to society. He, perhaps, may not be considered a pioneer in creating new forms of music, but was certainly a strong force in the spread of *dhrupad,* particularly.

Near the *Brija* land of Mathura and Brindavan, at Gwalior, Raja Man Singh Tomar, one of the most respected and generous patrons of *dhrupad,* reigned for nearly three decades from 1486 A.D. Under his enlightened support, *dhrupad* found a creative atmosphere for growth and his efforts were the cause of the production of many songs in the *Brij* dialect, modelled on those of Vidyapati. In his court were a galaxy of musicians such as Bakshu, Bhannu and Baiju and he was eulogized by Tansen who mentions him as one of his patrons.

The details of Haridas's life are not well known. There are two schools of thought. According to one he was born in 1480, A.D. in Rajpur, near Brindavan. His father's name was Gangadhar and his mother's Chitra Devi. At the age of twenty-five the youth was initiated into *sanyasa* by one Asudhir, belonging to the Nimbarka tradition. Haridas is said to have die in 1575 A.D. The second school holds that Haridas's father was Asudhir, a Saraswat Brahmin from Multan. Ganga Devi was his mother. The family migrated to a village called Khairwali Sarak, near Aligarh in Uttar Pradesh. Haridas was born here in 1512 A.D. and in his memory the place is now called Haridaspur. At the age of twenty-five the young man became a *sanyasi* and left his mortal coil in 1607 A.D.

In any case, the significant face was that from a very young age Haridas was drawn to the life of a recluse and became a *sanyasi*. He shifted his residence to Brindavan, the playground of the Immortal Cowherd and his beloved Radha. There he built his *asram* (hermitage) in Nidhuvan and sang his songs of the love of Radha-Krishna.

Swami Haridas's compositions may strictly be classed as *Vishnupadas*, that is, songs in praise of Lord Vishnu (Lord Krishna). But even his *prabandhas* which do not refer to Krishna have come to be known as *Vishnupadas*, perhaps because of the mystic source of his music; but they are musically constructed like *dhrupads*. He is also said to have composed *tirvats, ragamalas,* and such other forms. There are about 128 songs attributed to him, of which about eighteen are philosophical and a hundred and ten devotional. The former are known as *Siddhanta pada* and the latter as *Keli mala*.

Haridas was deeply learned and widely acquainted with the music of his days. He describes how Radha and Krishna are sporting. "Two beams of light are playing. Unique are their dance and music. *Ragas* and *raginis* of heavenly beauty are born. The two have sunk themselves in the ocean of *raga.*" Besides such descriptions, mention is found in his works of stringed instruments like *kinnari, aghouti,* of drums such as *mridang, daff.* He also talks of *ragas* like *Kedara, Gouri, Malhar* and *Vasant.*

The *swami* was not only a great musician but also a great teacher. The best known of his pupils was Tansen, one of the "nine gems" of Akbar's court. Tansen's tutelage with Swami Haridas is still a matter of tradition and popular belief; there is no incontrovertible proof that this was a fact. Also, neither Tansen's life nor his style of language show the religious depth of his master, if he did learn with Haridas at all. There is also a popular account that the renowned *dhrupad* singer and composer, Baiju, was contemporary to Tansen and a student of the *swami*. This, however, is doubtful.

The respect that Swami Haridas has received is not merely because of his musical genius, but also due to the literary beauty and simplicity of his *dhrupads*. More than anything else, his music and language were inspired by the mystic experience of *bhakti* and he is considered as one of the leading figures in the *bhakti* movement and music.

Swami Haridas belonged to the tradition of *madhura bhakti*—Adoration — expressed in erotic terms. It is said that he was deeply affected by the teachings of the Andhra philosopher and *bhakta,* Nimbarka (13th cent.), who sojourned in the North spreading the gospel of Radha-Krishna love. He propounded the philosophy of *bheda-abheda;* "the simultaneous difference and non-difference." But Haridas's theology goes further and embraces not merely the Love of Krishna and Radha but also the witnessing of the Love, a state of mind called *rasa.* This aspect of *rasa* is the theme of all his songs and teachings. In such an ecstatic conditon of trance he sings of the play of Krishna among the bowers of Brindavan; that is why, his Lord is known as *Kunj Bihari (Kunj*-bower, *bihari*-one who wanders). More than Krishna, Radha was the central personality of all his poems. He says, "Who knows of the quality of things more than Radha; if anyone has any knowledge at all, it is by her grace. None knows the beauty of *raga, tala* and the dance, as Radha does."

Swami Haridas began the *Haridasi* school of mysticism and had many spiritual disciples. The better known ones were Vitthal, Vipur, Viharin Deva, Krishna Das who fostered his tradition of devotional music. The main feature of this was that it was congregational. Groups of devotes came together and sang songs of the Lord of Brindavan. In the Brij district this congregation is called the *samaj* and is like the *sankeertan* of Bengal and the *bhajana gosti* of South India.

Though one of the greatest musicians of his times, the saint was completely indifferent to laurels and turned his face from all fame. Once Emperor Akbar wanted to hear him. It was impossible to bring the *Swami* to the royal court; and the hermitage was out of bounds to kings and such like. Therefore, Tansen thought of a ruse. Akbar would go in rags as a *tamboora* bearer with Tansen to Nidhuvan! The two went as planned and Emperor listened with rapt wonder to the divine music. On return to the court, Akbar remarked to Tansen, "How is it that with all your virtuosity, your music is so insipid compared to your *guru's?*" Tansen, replied, "What else can it be: for I sing to the Emperor of this land but he sings to the Emperor of Creation.

Tansen

Few musicians in North India have been extolled as Tansen. He has been described often as the greatest singer that this part of the country has known. Naturally, every school of musicians and almost every other Muslim musician claim to be descendents of this genius. So great an artist was he that even in his own times he became a legend. Abul Fazl, a contemporary of his, exclaims, "There has not been such a musician in the past thousand years, neither will there be another." But in spite of so much fame and renown, the facts of his life are not very definitely known, except in generalities; so much has been shrouded in myth. As a matter of fact, we are not even certain when he bceame a Muslim, if at all he did become one.

Makarand Pande (Mukundram Pande, Makarand Misra) was a Hindu priest, living in Behat village close to Gwalior and seems to have been proficient in music as well. While he begot many children, not one of them lived long. His neighbours advised him therefore, to seek the blessings of the Muslim saint of Gwalior, Hazrat Mohammad Ghouse. Accordingly, Pande travelled to the city and beseeched the *fakir* to bless him with a child. Ghouse was moved by the poor man's prayer and gave him a talisman to be tied round the neck of Pande's wife; and in due course the lady delivered a boy who was named Ramtanu. The lad was also called Tanna Misra. This Tanna Misra later on came to be better known to the world as Tansen. The year of his birth is not certain, though it is generally taken as 1506 A.D. (1520 or 1532). However, more recent studies have put his birth between 1492 or 1493 A.D.or, more generally, the last decade or two of the fifteenth century.

Again, the musical training of the renowned singer is not well documented. The usual tradition says that he was a disciple of Swami Haridas of Brindavan. The story of how the saint came across the boy Ramtanu goes thus: Once Swami Haridas and his students were on a pilgrimage and had to pass through a dense forest. As they went through the woods, they heard the fearful growls of a lion. Frightened for their lives the young boys ran as fast as their legs could carry them to the hermit for protection. He had his own doubts and sent them back to find out where the animal was hidden. As they quickly and with fear searched around, they came upon not a lion but a boy of ten perched on the branch of a tree and shouting at them like the animal. They caught hold of the naughty fellow, produced him before their master and told him of the incident. Haridas was impressed by the vocal 'talents' of the child who was none other than Ramtanu. The *Swami*, then, called for Makarand Pande and persuaded him to send the boy to Brindavan to study music. Thus Ramtanu became the disciple of Swami Haridas and learnt from him for many a long year. The tutelage of Tansen with the hermit of Brindavan is doubted by some; for they say that Tansen mentions nowhere in his *dhrupads* this fact; neither, it is contended, the language nor the spirit of his songs reflect those of Swami Haridas. Some are of the opinion that Ramtanu's early musical education was in a school of music established in Gwalior by Raja Man Singh and that he joined the *Swami* later on. It is surmised that Mohammad Ghouse was one of the teachers at this school. It is also said that at a later stage Tansen went to Bengal and for some time studied with Mohammad Shah Adil, the last king of the Suri Dynasty. After a few years of intense training he returned to Rewa to become the court musician of Raja Ramachandra. As for as Tansen's own account goes, no song of his mentions any *guru* other than Makarand.

A vocal music concert in Carnatic style

A vocal music concert in Hindustani style

Devotional singers from the north

Akashvani Vadya vrinda - the national orchestra of All India Radio

Folk singers of Kashmir in concert

Folk singers from Rajasthan in concert

Hari Prasad Churasia in concert

M.S. Gopalakrishnan in concert

V. Raghurama Ayyar in concert

M.S. Subbulakshmi in concert

Zakir Hussain in concert

Amjad Ali Khan in concert

Pt Vishnu Narayan Bhatkhanda

Pt Vishnu Digambar Paluskar

Rabindranath Tagore

There is a general belief that Ramtanu (Tanna Misra) became a convert to Islam. The tale is that recognizing the musical genius of the boy, his well-wishers took him to Hazrat Mohammad Ghouse for blessing. The *fakir,* with great affection for the child, put in his mouth a *beeda* (betel leaves and nut), half chewed by himself. While, of course, this action could be considered a benediction, it certainly made Tanna an outcast and a Muslim. According to another story, Tanna Misra became a Muslim in order to marry a girl of that religious belief. Rani Mriganayani, the widow of Raja Mansingh, was herself a good musician and Tanna was one of her favoured artists. The young man used to visit the palace often, both to listen to the queen as well as to sing to her. In the service of the *rani* there was a beautiful maid, Husini (a Hindu but converted to Islam). The lass and Tanna fell in love with each other and got married with the consent of the queen. The wedding was celebrated with Hazarat Mohammad Ghouse as the chief priest. It was for this ceremony that Tanna became a Muslim and from then on came to be called Ata Ali Khan.

Quite a number of scholars reject all this as meaningless, if not prejudiced ancedotes. First, it is pointed out that if Tanna's year of birth is taken as 1493 A.D., Mohammad Ghouse could have been a boy of only ten. Surely it would be absured to imagine that a child of ten could have blessed an elderly Brahmin, Makarand Pande, with a child! Also, the compositions of Tansen do not show any trace of Islamic influence; on the contrary, his devotion to Hindu gods is well known. Again, the rituals at his funeral were typically Hindu, a fact which casts further doubts on his ever having been converted to Islam. Added to all this is that no contemporary writer talks of such conversion.

Tanna Misra, in any case, was without doubt the most sought after musician of his days. Kings and Emperors vied with one another to keep him in their courts; it was such a signal honour and a prestige. His greatness as a singer was recognized early and Raja Vikramjit, the son of Raja Man Singh and ruler of Gwalior (1516-1518 A.D.), conferred upon the maestro the honorific title 'Tansen'. The first real patron of Tansen was Raja Ramchandra Baghela of Rewa. The king, an ardent admirer of the singer, is said to have given one crore golden coins to him in appreciation of his genius. The fame of the musician reached the ears of the young Emperor Akbar, through one Jain Khan. Raja Ramchandra had by this time become a subordinate king of the Moghul. He had perforce to agree to Akbar's request that Tansen be sent to the Imperial Court. The Emperor sent one Jalal Khan Kurchi with a posse of armed men to bring the great singer with all honours to his *darbar.* It must have been a painful separation for both. Tansen and

Raja Ramchandra. But the king bade him farewell and as a parting gift gave him a bracelet studded with priceless diamonds. Tansen bowed his head in gratitude and said, "Sire, this right hand of mine which is being honoured with these invaluable jewels will not receive any other honour from any other." So, it is said, he never took from then on any gift or present, from anybody, to be worn on his right hand. Thus, the unsurpassed *dhrupad* singer of all time entered as a highly respected courtier, the services of Emperor Akbar in 1562 A.D. and became famous as one of the "nine gems" of the Moghul Court.

In his old age Tansen returned to Gwalior where he died in the year 1595 A.D. (Other dates given for his demise are 1585, 1589 and 1610). His funeral was a memorable occasion, with a huge procession of song and dance, a characteristically Hindu custom. Before his passing away, he is said to have expressed a desire to be buried near the grave of Hazrat Mohammad Ghouse at Gwalior. This grave of his(?) has become a centre of pilgrimage to musicians and an annual festival is held there in memory of the immortal singer.

Tansen lived in a period when *dhrupad* reached its highest degree of popularity and so his compositions and style of singing were of this type. Both in their poetic beauty and musical grandeur they are some of the best songs we have. He is credited with thousands of *dhrupads,* a few hundreds of which bear the name of Akbar. Three works—Sangeet Sar, Raga Mala and Sri Ganesa Stotra—are attributed to him. Some of his *dhrupads* which have musical technicalities as their libretto (*sahitya*) reveal his profound insight into musical intricacies like *sruti, grama and moorcchana.* Tansen respectfully called *Miyan,* is traditionally accepted as the creator of new *ragas* which bear the prefix *Miyan*; *Miyanki Todi, Miyanki Sarang, Miyanki Malhar* and so on. *Raga Darbari Kanada,* musicians believe, is also his gift to the music of North India.

The musical descendants of *Miyan* Tansen have come to be known as the *Senia gharana.* One of his sons, Suratsen, specialized in *dhrupads* of *Dagar bani* and his progeny settled in Jaipur. Tansen's younger son Bilas Khan, continued his father's style of *Gauhar bani.* The daughter of the *Miyan,* Saraswati, married one Misri Singh who was a fine *veena* player and is considered to be the founder of an important school of instrumentalists of Hindustani music.

Sadarang

'Sadarang' holds the same pre-eminent position in the history of *kheyal* as does Tansen in the field of *dhrupad* and has been responsible for a new orientation in Hindustani music.

The origin of *kheyal* has often been a disputed subject. Many hold that Amir Khusro (13th cent.) was the originator of this style, mainly based on Persian modes. Others, on the contrary, are of the opinion that is was really a further elaborated development of the more ancient form called *sadharini geeta*. In any case, it became very popular during Muslim rule in North India, particularly during the reign of Sultan Hussein Saha Sharqui (later half of 15th cent.) who is said to have been responsible for the great revival of an encouragement to *kheyal*, But it was 'Sadarang' who placed it at the pinnacle of popularity it enjoys even to this day.

Sadarang was the signature of one Nyamat Khan, a court musician of the Mughal Emperor, Mohammad Shah (18th cent.). He is considered to be a descendant of Tansen through the latter's daughter, his father being Nirmol Khan (Lal Khan).

Nyamat Khan was originally a *veena* player and was unrivalled in his times. A *nawab* of Hyderabad who happened to visit Delhi in 1738 A.D. remarks, "Nyamat Khan is God's blessing to India... He is a master of *veena* and there has been no wizard of this instrument till now and it is doubtful if there will be one like him in the future". Besides being a rare instrumentalist, Nyamat Khan was also a very distinguished and talented singer of *dhrupad*. It is supposed that he studied music and literature with the poet Dev, a Tatari *qavval* and a Bengali musician named Natva.

Nyamat was attached to the court of Mohammad Shah 'Rangeele' as a *veena* player. It was a practice in those days for this instrument to be used to accompany singing (specially *dhrupad*), which meant that the player to sit behind the vocalist and be subordinate to him. This condition seems to have irked Nyamat Khan who must have considered himself equal to, if not better than, his contemporary musicians. He left the services of the King, therefore, unable to bear this state of affairs. Another story goes thus: Once, they say, Mohammad Shah felt that it would be fine to hear a duet of *sarangi* and *veena*. It was further decided that Nyamat Khan should play the *veena* and accordingly a courtier carried the royal command to the musician. Now, *sarangi* players were never considered 'respectable' and it was an unpardonable insult to the *veena* player to accompany a 'mean' *sarangi*. It was but natural that he flatly refused to obey the order. This threw the *Badshah* into a temper and he forthwith dismissed Nyamat Khan from the Court. Even Delhi city became too hot for Nyamat and he had to flee from the capital and live incognito for some time.

According to the tradition of his school of music, Nyamat Khan settled in Lucknow some time after 1719 A.D., and, as a kind of challenge, developed *kheyal* singing to a beautiful artistic quality. But he still chose to remain unknown. Here lived two young boys, Bahadur Khan and Dulle Khan (popularly known as the *Miyan* brothers), who were the sons of a famous *dhrupad* singer. Their father died when they were still children and the lads did not seem to have any liking to take to the profession of the family. Naturally, this came in for much taunting and criticism from their well wishers. So, one day, their mother took them to their uncle; but he rudely refused to teach them. It was then that she came to know of one Shah 'Sadarang'. Immediately, she went to him with a request that he kindly train the wayward boys. After much persuasion the maestro agreed and took them under his care and taught them his *kheyals*.

Nyamat Khan felt that, since he was from a family of *dhrupad* singers and *veena* players, he could not impart knowledge of *kheyal* to his family, for in those days it was *dhrupad* which was considered 'respectable' but not *kheyal*; no self-respecting musician would sing *kheyal* in public. Indeed, it is said that he never sang them in concerts. These he taught to his disciples. The *Miyan* brothers, therefore, studied *kheyals* with him and were acclaimed as unequalled. Their virtuosity was so great that they would set wagers in their performances. The young men would remove all their costly jewellery and throw them on the dias and challenge, "If any one can sing even this small *tan* of ours, these ornaments are his!". There were none to take on the bet!

Eventually the *Miyan* brothers got an opportunity to sing in the presence of King Mohammad Shah in Delhi. The ruler was immensely pleased with their new style and the beauty of the compositions and, on enquiry, came to know that their *ustad* (teacher), *Sadarang,* was none other than his erstwhile court musician, Nyamat Khan. Forgetting his old displeasure, he sent for the composer and appointed him once again in the court, with great honour. From then on Mohammad Shah's affection for Nyamat and his love for *kheyals* knew no bounds. Further, he requested him to teach his music also to the ladies of the palace.

This, perhaps, *Sadarang* did not like. He seems to have felt that such restrictions would only come in the way of his free life and musical development; Nyamat, hence, made a request that he be relieved of his duties in the court. It was not, of course, to the liking of his patron; however, the plea was agreed to on one condition; that *Sadarang* would always couple his name with that of the king in his compositons, thus perpetuating the memory.

of their association. Therefore, from then on Nyamat Khan used the signature *'Mohammad Shah—Sadarangeele'* . So, it is surmised, Nyamat Khan signed his songs in two ways; *Sadarang,* when he lived incognito in Lucknow and Mohammad Shah *Sadarangeela* when he rejoined the Delhi *darbar.*

In 'creating' the *kheyal* type, he must have experienced the gradual woodenness that had crept into his contemporary *dhrupad* with its more than mechanical insistence on arithmetical rhythm. As a departure from this bondage, eliminating the preliminary *alap,* he composed *kheyals* in simpler *talas* such as *Jhumra, Tilvada,* and *Ektal.* The melodic line was also made less severe with provision for variations and freer approach. In consonance with the ways of royal courts, their texts were also lyrical and often erotic. But they did maintain partly the dignity of *dhrupad,* without being tied down to a straight jacket. With changing times, many of these have become lower in structure and, perhaps, there is much of piracy and plagiarism in using his signature, *Sadarang.*

Nyamat Khan is said to have had two sons; Bhoopat Khan and Firoze Khan. The former's songs are signed *Maharang.* According to some, Firoze was not the son of *Sadarang*; but his nephew and son-in-law. He signed his *kheyal* as *Adarang* and was no mean composer himself. *Adarang* has given us many a *kheyal* of exquisitely chiselled beauty; but their content is more philosophical and religious in import. Also the songs are musically stricter in construction.

The last part of the 19th century saw a renaissance in Indian music and musicology throughout the country. There was a serious attempt to link the theories and practices of by gone centuries to current music. The need for such a search was particularly felt in North India, because of a great gap between the illiterate—but, of no inferior quality —artists and the grammarians. The situation was not a very happy one. But Vishnu Narayan Bhatkhande and Vishnu Digambar Paluskar, two gigantic personalities, appeared on the scene and gave a new direction to Hindustani music, specially to its theoretical and social aspects.

Vishnu Narayan Bhatkhande

Narayan Bhatkhande was a clerk in Bombay, working with a trader. He had a house in Walkeswar, a part of the metropolitan city. There Narayan Rao lived with his family—a wife and five children. Vishnu, the second child of his parents, was born on August 10, 1860 (the *Janmastami* day, birth day of Lord Krishna) Though named Vishnu, he was usually called Gajanan, or affectionately Anna (elder brother). Like boys in a middle class family, he was put to a Marathi school and later into the Elphinstone High School. This school was about three miles from his residence and Gajanan had to go and come on foot, for there were neither trams nor buses in those days and the family could not afford a bicycle.

Vishnu had a fine physique and personality, and was, therefore, very popular among his companions. By 1885 he had graduated from the Elphinstone College and in 1887 completed the course in Law. His married life was a short one; for within a few years after marriage both his wife and the only daughter passed away. Vishnu was alone and music became, from then on, his only love and mission.

Interest in music came to Bhatkhande early in life. By about the age of ten he could play the flute with some competence, and was a popular artiste in the local festivities. During his college days, he started learning *sitar*. But it was not an age which encouraged 'respectable' families to take to music, except listening to it from a safe distance. So, Vishnu had to go to study the instrument on the sly, without the knowledge of his parents.

There was in the neighbourhood, one Gopal Giri who was a *sitar* player and Anna, on hearing him, decided to train himself to play this lute. Gopal Giri took the young man to his own teacher, Vallabhacharya Damulji. Vallabhdas was a blind but rich man and had no need to earn his livelihood. He was considered a very good player on *sitar*. On Vishnu meeting him, he said, "This music is a hard taskmistress. How can you study music, if you are also going to the college?" But the boy's enthusiasm touched Damulji and finally the master allowed him to come and listen to him. After a few months he began to teach the eager pupil. Vishnu had to go to Vallabhdas' house at night and secretly practised there. Thus he continued for a few years; but eventually people came to know of this young sitarist. He started playing at small soirees in the homes of friends. In one such performance Gajanan's father also turned up, much to the shock of the son. Narayan did not know that the day's artiste was to be Vishnu; neither was the boy aware that his father had been invited to the soiree. It must have been awkward for both. Narayan Bhatkhande heard his son's playing and liked it. Returning home, he told his wife about the incident and Vishnu's interest in music. They decided, fortunately, not to come in the way of their son's musical training. Anna was, therefore permitted to continue it on the condition that it did not disturb his academic work.

Some rich Parsi and Gujarati patrons had started an organization, Gayan Uttejak Mandali, where concerts by distinguished musicians were held. There were also classes arranged for interested students in music. Bhatkhande soon joined the Mandali and even became a keen learner. He studied *dhrupad* with Raoji Bua Belbagkar and *kheyal* with Ali Hussein, both of whom were working there. This also gave an opportunity to come into contact with many a great artiste, the best known of them being the Bhindi Bazar family headed by Chajju Khan.

For nearly fifteen years Bhatkhande was associated with the Mandali. Though he learned the practical art, and listened to much, one fact constantly came up in his mind; the lack of any cogent theory and codification in Hindustani music. No doubt the performers were great; but many of them did not have any clue to the grammar of what they were singing or playing. So, on his own, he studied various books and old manuscripts—whatever were available. He also felt deeply that the more educated class of society should take a serious interest in music—its practice and theory.

While continuing in his profession of law, from which he retired in 1910, he started on a series of visits to various places in India to gather as much knowledge of music as he could get. Bhatkhande went to Gujarat, Saurashtra, Bengal, Madras and to many other areas. He met musicians, perused books and manuscripts, and learnt without prejudice all that came his way. Later on, he even edited and published some of these. While at Ettiayapuram in South India he met the renowned pioneer musicologist, Subbarama Dikshitar, the author of *Sangeeta Sampradaya Pradarsini*, one of the most comprehensive and standard books of scored songs. Bhatkhande's tours to East and North brought him into contact with traditional musicians from whom he gathered compositions in rare and common *ragas*. His perigrinations in North India, particularly to Rampur, had a great influence on his musical practice and concepts. Rampur, a tiny state, was then known for its galaxy of musicians. Wazir Khan, the *veena* player, Mohammad Ali Khan, the *rabab* player, Kale Nazir Khan, the vocalist were among the famous court musicians of the Nawab. Nawab Ali Khan, the ruler, was himself an accomplished musician and his cousin, Sadat Ali Khan (more popularly known as Chamman Sahab) was an expert player of *sur singar,* a plucked stringed instrument. Bhatkhande learnt much from these and their contribution to his repertoire was of no mean extent.

Vishnu Bhatkhande was one of the first to organize a full-fledged conference of musicians and musicologists. Better known for their predilections of differences than to common and fair discussions, it was no easy matter to bring musicians to one platform. But he was fortunate in having the support and encouragement of Maharaja Sayaji Rao of Baroda. Eminent artistes from many parts of the country participated; research papers were read by scholars like Clements, Deval and others. The gathering itself was presided over by no less a person than Raja Nawab Ali Khan, Indeed, the *raja* later summarised and published the ideas of Bhatkhande in Urdu in the book, *Marif-un-Naghmat.*

Maharaja Sayaji Rao was a highly cultured ruler and was anxious that there should be a proper centre for training in music. On his request, Bhatkhande reorganized the Baroda state Music School, with Hirjibhai Doctor as the Principal. Eventually this school became the nucleus for the Music College of M.S. University of Baroda and had the distinction of having on its staff Ustad Fayyaz Hussein Khan, Ustad Nissar Hussein Khan and such other very eminent personalities.

Maharaj Scindia of Gwalior had came to know of the services of this savant. Gwalior, one of the greatest centres of Hindustani music, had many fine musicians but no organized school. Bhatkhande was, therefore, approached by the Scindia to help him in founding an institution for training in music. Many singers from Gwalior were sent to Bombay to stay with Bhatkhande so that they could learn his methods of musical pedagogy; and with the help of these traditional musicians, guided by Bhatkhande, the Madhav Music College was established in Gwalior in 1918.

One of Bhatkhande's intense ambitions was to found and run a music college of really high standards. The idea was broached in many music conferences convened by him; a number of people pledged their support, but nothing came out of these efforts. However, the Fifth All India Music Conference at Lucknow in 1925, examined ways and means of setting up a well-planned College; and in 1926 the Marris College of Music, one of the premier institutions of its kind then, was started in Lucknow. Many a distinguished musician and scholar gave selflessly of his services to this College. Today it has grown larger in stature and has been renamed the Bhatkhande College of Music, in memory of this great man.

The monumental contribution of this pioneer was his collection and publication of compositions in Hindustani music. He must have spent much in time, energy and money to acquire them. Bhatkhande had even to design a system of notation to write these down. All this was not easy, for the reserve and unwillingness of most musicians to part with their knowledge is proverbial. But he did not give up; he continued undaunted and published about 1000 songs of tradition, apart from 300 of his own (he used the signature *'Chatur'*) in six volumes, known as the *Kramik Pustak Malika.* A keen intellect, he could not rest with this; being aware of a chasm between theory and practice, he penned the famous *Hindustani Sangeet Paddhati* of nearly 2,500 pages, in four volumes, in the Marathi language. He was also the author of works like *Sreemallaksya Sangeetam,, Abhinava Raga Manjari* (both in Sanskrit) and edited various classics. Other important contributions were, *A Short Historical Survey of the Music of Upper India* and *A Comparative Study of Some of the Leading Systems of Music of the 15th, 16th, 17th and 18th centuries.* The schemes of classification of *ragas* into ten *thatas* (parental scales) is also his and is now the most popular in North India.

Pandit Vishnu Narayan Bhatkhande was struck with paralysis and after protracted illness of three years, expired on September 19, 1936 (the day of *Ganesh Chaturthi*).

There has been severe criticism—quite often justified—of his work and concepts. It is said that the compositions which he published were not always correct in text and notation. His theory of *srutis* is considered very much off the mark. The idea of the ten parent scales is not without serious faults. Much of all this may be true; but it must be borne in mind that the period of his life and work was one of obscurantism and obdurate orthodoxy. That Bhatkhande could do all this at all is a tribute to this man and one wonders whether such an enormous task could have been accomplished by one mortal.

Vishnu Digambar Paluskar

The Gadgils were a family of Brahmins in the village, Palus, in Maharashtra. One of them is said to have had a vision of the Divine and blessed by it and so from then on this family became something special and came to be known as the Paluskars, the original name being forgotten. Into this family, Vishnu Digamber was born on August 18, 1872 at Kurundwad, the principal town of an Indian 'native' state; those were the days of British rule.

Vishnu's father, Digambar Gopal Paluskar, was a *Keertankar* (singer of *Keertan*—a religious discourse). *Keertan* in Maharashtra, like the *Harikatha Kalakshepam* in South India, is a kind of story-telling of *Puranic* legends, in song, verse and prose; Digambar was one such singer of *Puranas*. Vishnu, naturally, from childhood acquired a taste and bent for singing, as he accompanied his father during the latter's concerts. He was also studying at a local school in Kurundwad, due to the kind interest taken in the young boy by the *Raja* of the principality.

Near Kurundwad, is a small town called Narsobachi Wadi where every year a festival, *Datta Jayanti,* is celebrated with great eclat—fireworks and all. Vishnu, like millions of others, was an active participant; on one such occasion of merriment a cracker burst near his face, damaging his eyes permanently. No treatment at Kurundwad was of any avail; the boy was then sent to the neighbouring town, Miraj, where the royal physician, Dr. Bhadbhade tried his best but failed to restore vision to the poor lad.

Both the avenues—academic studies and that of *keertankar*—were cut off to Vishnu. Dr. Bhadbhade, who had listened to the boy's devotional songs felt that he could blossom out into a musician. With the consent of Digambar Paluskar, he spoke to the Raja of Miraj. The ruler was quick to realize the talents of the child and put him under the guidance of Balakrishna Bua Ichalkaranjikar.

Balakrishna Bua was the doyen of musicians in Maharashtra. The grand old man had learnt singing in Gwalior under eminent masters and was highly respected for his knowledge of the art. Paluskar studied with him till about 1896. It was a hard and strenuous discipleship, for there were no regular courses, no regular lessons and everything depended on the moods of the teacher. Besides, one had to do all the household chores for the *guru* and his family. This kind of apprenticeship—*gurukula vasa*—was difficult but paid dividends in the long run. Vshnu was very successful and this, perhaps, raised the ire in his fellow students. They were all the more jealous of him, for he was quite intimate with the royal family, which they were not. It is possible that they poisoned the Bua's mind against Vishnu; in any case, the relation between the two became strained. So Paluskar along with two of his friends, left Miraj; and after visiting many places reached Baroda. This city like Gwalior was then a well-known seat of learning and art, and he decided to settle there. News of the arrival of a young singer and his attractive music slowly reached the Maharaj. In course of time an invitation to sing at the Court came and he gave a commendable performance in the royal presence. The Maharani was pleased with the young man and presented him with lavish gifts and a friendly warning—he better leave Baroda as local musicians were becoming too envious for him to be safe!.

From there he toured Saurashtra, Gwalior, Mathura, Bharatpur, Delhi and reached Punjab. While in Saurashtra he gave a public concert charging a nominal fee—a scandalous thing to do and a complete departure form tradition. For traditionally concerts were always either in the chambers of a rich patron or in a temple. While at Mathura he studied the *Brij* dialect in which exist some of the finest compositions in Hindustani music and this helped to a great extent his understanding the beauty of the language of these songs.

Punjab was really the starting point of the most significant aspect of Vishnu Digambar's life. He lived in Amritsar for some time, but soon shifted to Okara in Montgomery District to be the tutor of Sir Khemsingh's children. After a few months of stay there, he came to Lahore; and here on May 5, 1901 he founded the Gandharva Mahavidyalaya. This is one of the most interesting turning points in the history of modern music, as it was the first school run by a middle class musician without the direct patronage of *rajas* and *maharajas*. The Vidyalaya (school) was run by public support, donations from the richer classes and funds raised by the concerts of Vishnu Digambar— it was truly a school of the people for the people.

Here he brought together a set of pupils whom he trained not only in music, but also inculcated in them a respect for the art and a missionary zeal. This group of his early students became later some of the most distinguished performers and teachers in North India. What was more important was the atmosphere in the institution; while there was strict discipline in musical training, there was stricter discipline in moral training. The usual odium attached to the clan of musicians was thus removed and they began to be treated with respect.

Paluskar now felt that his activities needed expansion and, therefore, came to Bombay in September, 1908 to found a branch of the Gandharva Mahavidyalaya there. Gradually, as the work in this city increased, the school at Lahore was shifted to Bombay. Even the printing press which he had established in Lahore to print books in music was taken over to the new precincts. Vishnu Digambar's fame as a teacher spread and hundreds of students began to pour into his *Vidyalaya*.

Before long it became necessary to increase facilities for teaching. With the help of loans from friends, a building to house the Gandharva Mahavidyalaya was built in 1915. A little later even a hostel for students was constructed. All this involved considerable borrowing of money and Paluskar came under huge debts. Even with the best of efforts it became almost impossible for him to discharge the loans. He gave concerts at various places to collect the necessary funds but this never fetched him sufficient money. In 1924, when he was on a concert tour, his creditors attached his properties and auctioned them to realize their debts. Paluskar must have been a heart-broken man after this. The cause for which he had struggled so far received an irretrievable set-back. He had, however, one satisfaction: he had created a number of zealous disciples who went to almost every region of the land, established schools and taught selflessly.

Even while in Bombay, Vishnu Paluskar had started *Sri Ram Nam Adhar Ashram* in Nasik; to this hermitage he moved in 1924. From this as centre he travelled widely in India and Nepal. But his health was running down and the Raja of Miraj shifted the ailing musician to Miraj, the town which had seen the rise of Paluskar's career. There he passed away on August 21, 1931 to the music of the sacred chant of Rama's name.

The domestic life of Vishnu Digambar was disappointing in a sense. Of his three sisters, one had become a widow and lived with him, along with her children. He had twelve of his own; but all of them except one died young. The last, a son, was Dattatreya. Even he could not get the advantage of studying with his father, for Vishnu Digambar died when the boy was only eleven years of age. Dattatreya later came under the care of the senior pupils of Paluskar and grew into a very highly promising singer. But as ill-fate would have it, Dattatreya Vishnu Paluskar died young suddenly in 1955.

Vishnu Digambar Paluskar was a towering figure in the field of music; a musician of a high order, a great teacher, a man of uncompromising moral courage and a soul imbued with the awareness of the social values of art.

As an artiste he was a very popular and successful one. The training he had had with the great Ichalkaranjikar was a thorough one and Paluskar himself was endowed with an attractive voice and musical sensitivity. His apprenticeship under his father as *keertankar* might have given him a sense of the dramatic in artistic presentation. Whereever he went, he drew an appreciative audience and was honoured by princely patrons. But characteristically, he spent all the fortune he amassed to further the cause of music. More than any other aspect of his musical career—which was dynamic in every direction—was his deeply religious approach to the art. To him music was a path to God-realization and could not be divorced from moral commitments. The ways that most musicians lived were far from clean. The texts of songs even in *kheyals* were sometimes nauseating—and even today one cannot often meet *kheyals* of really good poetic worth in Hindustani music. Paluskar felt that these kept the more intelligent section of society away from music. To remedy the situation, he brought in strict living and behaviour in his school. His own conduct was above reproach and he saw to it that his students were of exemplary character. As for the songs, he either composed new ones with cleaner content or altered the words of older ones, keeping their tunes unchanged. These efforts gradually had their effect. More and more students—particularly girls—came out to join his Vidyalaya: society began to feel that even if music was not a very paying profession, it, at least, was not a debasing one. Towards the end of his life his time was devoted almost entirely to religious music and finally his end also came amidst the singing of *Ram dhun* (Rama's name).

With very few exceptions, Paluskar was undoubtedly the most renowned teacher of music of recent times. Many great musicians were not necessarily great teachers and many well-known *ustads* and *pandits* were not necessarily fine musicians. But Vishnu Digambar was both an artiste and a teacher of high order. His most notable task was the opening of the musical world to amateurs, for traditionally it was almost impossible for outsiders to enter into the clannish monopolies of the *ustads*. Paluskar himself had learnt music the hard way and must have seen the inordinate wastage of time and energy on the part of the student in non-musical activities of 'serving' the *guru*. He, therefore, founded schools which ran on regular syllabi. Books with notations of songs to help the student were published. Theory of music was taught on a systematic basis. It was the pioneering efforts of Paluskar and Bhatkhande that have become the incentive for music to be considered academic enough to be included in the courses of studies in universities. Institutionalizing musical training has been the most significant trend set by these two savants. Obviously, all this was well intentioned. But whether it really has been creatively effective is a question that is raised in many quarters; for, often, it is felt and said that it has spread an interest in the art but has lessened the depth of understanding.

It was an era when musicians were socially looked down upon. They were illiterate, uncouth and immoral, Paluskar had bitter experiences of his own *guru* being treated in a disdainful manner. He was determined to show to the world that musicians were as good and great as anyone else! It is said that a *maharaja* wanted to listen to Vishnu Digambar and fixed a time for the soiree, at the musician's house. At the appointed time, the king and his retinue gathered and the singer began. After a while, the ruler, wanting to smoke and lighted his cigar. To Paluskar it was not only unpleasant but an insult. Being blind, he did not know who was smoking, but, in any case, he ordered that the smoking be stopped. The embarassed aide whispered into his cars, "How can it be? It is the *maharaja* and I dare not ask him to desist". Paluskar exclaimed, "What do you mean by *maharaja*; I am the *maharaja* in my room! Ask him to stop it or get out."

More than anything, Vishnu Digambar's contribution is to the social values attached to music and musicians. An art which was once held sacred, as a royal road to realization, a science which was the fifth Veda, had fallen into bad days. It had taken to nothing but Bohemian pleasures—almost— and musicians were, apart from being musicians, not welcome as very pleasant citizens. Paluskar had to fight against the orthodoxy of the 'elite' who looked askance at the art and artistes and against the professionals who would not step out of their secretive guilds. It was an ardous, thankless and challenging task. But he did succeed. He was able to persuade society that music was a *fine* art and musicians were not necessarily a despicable tribe. Great social and political men of his time like Gopala Krishna Gokhale, Mrs. Annie Besant and Mahatma Gandhi recognized his missionary work and social awareness. Paluskar's *Ram dhun, "Raghupati Raghava Raja Ram"* was sung at the head of the famous Dandi March led by Gandhiji in 1930 and his *"Vande Mataram"* was invariably heard at the sessions of the then Indian National Congress. Thanks to Paluskar, today one can become a musician without having to bow his head in shame.

Purandaradasa

As with most of Indian personalities, the historical aspects of life are rarely important; for few of them or their contemporaries leave sufficient factual details recorded. While this attitude stems from a realization of the unimportance of the individual in the magnitude of creation, it, all the same builds up often unbelieveable myths round such great people. Purandaradasa is no exception.

To the extent we can gather from available facts, the *dasa* was born in a place called Purandaralaya ghatta (Purandara pura, Purandara ghatta)—the whereabouts of which is not yet decided—or somewhere near Hampi, the then capital of the Vijayanagara Empire; both are in Karnatak. He lived probably from 1480 to 1564 A.D. His father was one Varadappa Nayaka or Vittala Nayaka. Before he was ordained as a *dasa*, when he was in his late thirties, he was called Sreenivasa Nayaka or Krishnappa Nayaka and was married to one Saraswati Bai (Gautami Bai?) They had four boys (three according to some) and perhaps a daughter.

While these are the bare details of his life, the popular lore goes thus:

Varadappa Nayaka was a very wealthy jeweller of Purandaragarh in the south of the present day Maharashtra. To him was born in 1484 A.D. a son who was named Sreenivasa, affectionately called Seenappa or Timmappa. Seenappa was born, as the saying goes, with a silver spoon in his mouth. By his own efforts he enhanced the family wealth to immense proportions. With an astute mind, obstinate and miserly, Seenappa became one of the most well-known jewellers and came to be called 'Navakoti Narayana'—an appellation for a multi-millionire. However, he happened to be also a great scholar and musician.

But his notoriety as an impossible miser was a pain not only to his friends (if he had any at all!) but also to his wife, Saraswati Bai. But she could do nothing to convert him, an extremely pious and generous lady though she was.

One day a Brahman came to him for monetary assistance to meet the expenses of some religious ceremony. "Come tomorrow", was the answer. The Brahman came the next day and received the same answer. The poor fellow realized that he had little chances of getting even an old counterfeit coin from the miser. So, when Seenappa was at his shop, the Brahman, went to Saraswati Bai. Unfortunately, the lady had no money to give him, as her husband would leave the house only after leaving everything in the house locked safely. Helpless and in desperation, she took out her diamond nose-ring and told the gentleman to sell the ornament and use the money so realized. Off went the man straight to Seenappa to sell it. One can imagine the money-lender's reaction. He at once knew that the jewel was his wife's. "She had no business to be generous," he thought. Sreenivasa told the Brahman to wait and went directly home in a fury and asked Saraswati Bai to show him the nose-ring. Poor lady! She did not know what to do. She requested Seenappa to wait, telling him that she had left it in the bathroom. Going to the prayer room, instead, she prayed to the Lord. Determining to end her life, for she was only too familiar with her husband's wrath, she lifted a cup of poison to her lips. And what did she find but the jewel in the cup. She came and gave it to the impatient man. He was speechless and hastened to his shop; looking into the safe, he could not find the nose-ring there. Running back home, Seenappa heard from his wife the whole story. Truly a moment of epiphany and Revelation.

Forthwith Sreenivasa renounced his wealth. He was as severe in giving up his worldly accumulation as in gaining it. With his wife and children he became a mendicant, penniless, wandering in search of something which would give him peace. A man of strong will, he would not rest till he found his guru, someone who could show the path of Truth.

Finally, he met Vyasaraya, the royal guru of Vijayanagara Emperors and one of the profoundest *yogis* of that era. Vyasaraya initiated him and from then on Seenappa became a member of the order of *Haridasas*, the servants of the Lord. Seenappa died to the world and Purandaradasa was born; and with the exception of Kanakadasa, the goatherd, no other *dasa* is revered as Purandara is. His writings and songs have come to be called *Purandara Upanishad*. Even his guru exclaimed, "If ever there is a *dasa*, it is Purandara". The *dasa* travelled widely to Nanjangud, Belur, Udupi, Pandharpur and other holy places and composed songs on the deities. The learning and *bhakti* of the saint, but even more the respect that Vyasaraya had for Purandara, made the pundits of the monastery jealous. What was more scandalous to them was that the guru had placed the writings of Purandara on the top of a stack of sacred books. There could be nothing more sacrilegious!. So one of the inmates threw away the manuscripts of Purandara. But miraculously, they flew back and landed on top of the file of books. This happened twice. Vyasaraya could but smile at the philistine. Such then was Purandaradasa, the like of whom comes once in few centuries; and even the divine bard, Tyagaraja bowed his head in humility to the *dasa* or *dasas*. After an unbelievably creative life Purandaradasa attained *samadhi* in 1564, at the age of eighty.

The *dasas* were a kind of wandering ministrels carrying the word of the love of the Lord from door to door. The finest experiences of mystics often got caught up in books and words. Even these sometimes were not accessible to all, as they became closely guarded 'secrets' of certain types of 'learned' people. At such times of ignorance came the *dasas*, the servants and messengers of the Lord, who were themselves great mystics, and communicated to every one the beauty of Adoration in the language that everyone could understand. Such a one was Purandaradasa who sang of the deeply religious life in the simplest of words.

The burden of much of what he said was the feeling of complete surrender. He says, "Knowing of my plight, Lord or Lords, why dost thou forsake me? I have no relatives, I have no friends; I have no father, no mother. Thou art my father, Thou art my mother and Thou art my relative. Eternally do I have my trust in thee, Krishna". For him, as to all who have experienced the essential, the ceremonial religion without self-effacement was worthless. "Such a religion is a show and such 'saints' are saints of the stomach; all for the guarantee of a square meal". Social differences were meaningless. "Who is the untouchable? Is he the one outside the village? Is he not amongst the 'respected. people?. He who has, but does not give in charity is the untouchable; he who does not speak gently is the untouchable; he who thinks only of 'I' is the worst untouchable".

The literary beauty of Purandaradasa's compositions is indeed of the highest order. He talks of the power of *Nama* (Numen), the praise of guru, inner experiences, social problems, true religion and so on. The style is simple and easy but extremely effective. With similies from daily life, he brings home his point with ruthless honesty. "Art Thou not called the lover of the devotees; then why dost thou not obey them?—Thus he commands the Lord. "If a thief sees a purse in the mirror and makes a hole in the mirror to get it will it become his?". "What use is it to keep the bitter *Neem* in sweet jaggery; what use it for a deceitful mind to utter sweet *mantra*?"

Besides the greatness of feeling and delicate style of literary expression, Purandara's music was the most effective form of communication. He had intended to compose 5,00,000 songs, dealing with holy places, eulogy of guru, *tantra, mantra,* rituals, devotional songs and so on. But it is said that he could complete only 4,75,000 of them. Even if it is assumed that he commenced composing at the young age of fifteen and continued till the time of his demise, this would work out an average of twenty songs a day; an almost superhuman phenomenon. The rest of the songs, 25,000 of them, legend has it, were completed by Vijayadasa (17th-18th cent.), who was supposed to have been the reincarnation of Purandara's son, Madhavapati, and initiated in a dream by the great saint himself. Besides the enormity of the number, the variety is also staggering—*padas, suladis, ugabhogas* and *devara namas.* It is an indescribable tragedy that much of this is lost to us; indeed, we have lost even the original music of these works and there is no authentic record or tradition of singing them.

Apart from being a supreme artist, he was a pioneer in musical pedagogy, for he is said to have standardized and brought into order teaching methods in music. One of the most significant innovations he made was the postulation of *Maya mala-vagaula* (C Db E F G Ab B)— Sa ri Ga Ma Pa dha Ni—as the standard scale for teaching. To this day it is the first *raga* taught to beginners in South India. Purandara also developed graded lessons of *savaravali* (preliminary scale exercise), *janta varisai* (exercises with paired notes), *alankara* (note patterns) and *pillari geeta* (small songs) to train students in the intricacies of music. Therefore he has been reverently called the *Adi guru* (the first guru) and *Karnataka Sangeeta Pitamaha* (the father of Carnatic music). But to him music was prayer. "There should be rhythm, and tune; but there should be peace .... The voice should be faultless; the words should be clear; there should be no confusion; the mien must be radiant. The learned must be there to listen and there should be great happiness. Ah, but you must sing that Purandara Vitthala is the Lord of Lords".

Kshetrayya

What Jayadeva is to Sanskrit poetry and North Indian music, Kshetrayya is to Telugu and South Indian music. The same abandon, and the same delicateness of feeling run through the works of the two poet-musicians.

Very scanty and indefinite are the known facts of Kshetrayya's life. As a matter of fact, the real name of this musician was Varadayya and Kshetrayya (Kshetrajna) was a later appellation. This much is known that he was born in the 17th century in Andhra.

There are many versions of his life's story. According to one, Varadayya became a peripatetic saint, initiated by a *yogi*. He began composing *padams* on God Gopala of Muvva. He took to wandering from place to place, visiting the courts of kings and *nawabs,* and holy centres (*kshetras*); hence the name *Kshetrayya* or *Kshetrajna.* Another opinion is that he was, in the beginning, a courtier and wrote *padams* for the pleasures of kings and their harems. On his return to Muvva, after his tours to Thanjavur and other towns, he fell in love with *devadasi.* She, however, spurned his advances, saying that she would not consent to live with a singer who sang of mere earthlings and that too far worldly considerations. So, Varadayya retired to the temple and meditated therein till he had the divine vision. He became a changed man and along with the *devadasi* roamed about singing songs in praise of Lord Gopala. A third tradition runs as follows: Varada was an illiterate cowherd, but a devotee of Gopala in Muvva village. He loved a young milkmaid in the hamlet. But his lack of any literary culture was a handicap to their union! Therefore, he went into a deep meditation and Gopala blessed him with the power of words and song. The maid accepted him and together they wandered singing his lyrics on Muvva Gopala.

Varadayya or Kshetrayya and his lady made their way from town to town, village to village. It is known that he was a welcome visitor to the court of Raghunatha Nayak of Tanjavur. Varada talks of having sung more than four thousand *padams* and that, in a contest, composed fifteen hundred of them in forty days. After a long perigrination he finally reached Kanchipuram and nothing is known of him thereafter.

One cannot be very sure whether the music of his *padams* which we now hear is the original as Kshetrayya gave them. But these songs do cast a magical spell with the dignity of tune and simple lyricism of words and they have lent themselves to dance as few other *padams* have. The language is strikingly direct and rustic with immediate appeal. All the songs cry of the pangs of the women for union with the Lord; the pain of separation, the consuming jealousy and suspicion, the memory of happy moments—in short, all that is involved in love is detailed with stark frankness but without a touch of the obscene. And Kshetrayya is himself the woman beseeching for the Grace of the Infinite. The allegoric love of the heroine to Muvva Gopala (which, incidentally, is also his signature), Lord Krishna, is as real at the physical plane as the mystic and the excellence of communication is equalled by few.

The Trinity

Syama Sastri, Tyagaraja and Muthuswami Dikshitar have been aptly called the *Trimoorty* (Trinity) of Carnatic music, in analogy to the three

Facets of Godhead. Truly, one cannot think of many composer-singers who have been so creative. The most surprising fact is that they were all contemporaries and were born in the same village, Tiruvarur, in the Thanjavur District of South India. All of their ancestors migrated from the northern areas of this part of the country and each in his unique way has contributed to the enrichment of South Indian Music. A new era was ushered in with the coming of these three saintly singers.

Syama Sastry

A group of Vadama Brahmins of Kambham in Andhra left their native land and migrated to Kanchipuram in Tamil Nadu, for those were days of military invasions from the northern parts of the Deccan and life was more secure down south.

In Kanchipuram had been installed a golden idol of Goddess Kamakshi—it is said, by Lord Brahma Himself. The idol was known as *Bangaru* (Golden) Kamakshi. When that immortal mystic and philosopher, Sri Adi Sankaracharya, visited the town, he saw the miserable condition of the temple. Having got it renovated and put into order, he chose this family from Kambham to be the priests of the temple.

But life even here was precarious, after the fall of the Vijayanagara Empire at the end of the 16th cent, and many a family migrated to safer enclaves. The Kambham priests, therefore, left Kanchipuram with the image of *Bangaru* Kamakshi and their valuables hidden in a drum. Eventually they reached Gingee, and were protected and honoured by the local ruler. We see their descendants later in Udayampalayam, by the end of 17th century, and some time after in Tiruvarur.

Of this lineage was Viswanatha Iyer who was in the service of Raja Tulajaji for some period and was a priest by profession. To him was born on 26th April 1762 a son who was named Venkatasubramania, later to be better known as Syama Sastry. As was the custom, he was taught Sanskrit, Telugu and a little music. When Venkatasubramania was eighteen, Viswanatha Iyer shifted to Tanjavur.

The family were not musicians by profession; neither were they inclined to train the boy in that art and, perhaps, were planning to make him also a priest. Fate, however, intervened in the guise of one *Sangeeta Swami,* a recluse from Andhra. While this *sanyasi* was at Thanjavur, Viswanatha Iyer invited him to his house and presented his son before him. The *swami* knew of the gifts of the youth and perhaps what the future held for him. So he requested the father to send Syama to him for training in music. After a rigorous study, the guru suggested that the boy should associate himself with Pacchimiriyam Adiyappayya, the court musician of Tanjavur. From then on a deep, affectionate friendship grew between Venkatasubramania and Adiyappayya though they were a generation apart in age.

Syama Sastry was a scholar, a pious priest and a composer of great merit. He was also occultly advanced, specially in *tantra,* a particular *yogic path.* It is believed that it was he who initiated his junior contemporary, Muthuswami Dikshitar, into *Sri Vidya,* a form of worship of the Goddess. Both materially, for he seems to have been well to do, and mentally he did not need any royal patronage. By nature he was aloof and contented himself with himself. He kept the company of scholars and musicians; and amongst them was the immortal Tyagaraja whom he visited often at Tiruvayyaru.

Though Syama Sastry was a great composer, his works have not received as wide an acclaim as those of the other two of the Trinity. Tyagaraja's music has an emotional appeal coupled with technical viability which can touch the lay and the learned alike. Dikshitar's compositions, though most dignified and possibly the most difficult of the three, has yet a tradition mainly because of his brothers, their descendants and pupils. Syama Sastry, whose signature was *Syamakrishna*, was more intricate and difficult in his musical technique, particularly the rhythmic aspect. He did not, perhaps, care to teach any student and thus his songs are sung less often than those of the other two. His mastery over *tala* has become too well known to be emphasised here, and his defeating the redoubtable Kesavayya is a much publicised legend. This Kesavayya of Bobbili (in Andhra) has called himself, '*Bhooloka chapa chutti Kesavayya*', that is 'Kesavayya who could roll the world into a mat'. In one of his all-conquering itinerant musical contests, he came to Tanjavur. No musician of the town dared to meet him in a competition and they had to beseech Syama Sastry to take up the gauntlet. Sastry not only accepted the challenge but sang a *pallavi* in *Sarabhanandana tala* which had 79 *aksaras* to a cycle, with complicated internal divisions. Kesavayya could not match this performance and was duly declared defeated!

Syama Sastry passed away on February 16, 1827. Of his descendants, his second son, Subbaraya Sastry (1803-1862), was a composer of merit and has left us many fine works.

Tyagaraja

"On whose art no human hand can improve".

The life and work of Tyagaraja, the bard of Tiruvayyaru, is a miracle of miracles. For no musician, with the exception of Purandaradasa, revolutionized and gave a new direction to Indian music as he did. So creative a musician and saint was he that he has come to be known as *Sri Tyaga Brahmam*, which is a reference not only to his creativity but carries with it a part of his father's name, Ramabrahmam.

The bulwark of a great culture, the Vijayanagara Empire, with all its glory, fell at the end of the 16th century. The invasion from the North brought in its wake new, though not always commendable, trends in living. Quite a few Hindu families had to flee to Southern areas which were still peaceful. Many found shelter under the benign rule of the Nayakas and the Maratha kings of Tamilnadu. Particularly, a number of Telugu families went South and formed nuclei of art and culture. Tyagaraja's ancestors belonged to one such stock, as he describes himself as descending from the Kakarla family. (Kakarla is a village in the Kurnool District of Andhra.)

Tiruvarur in the Tanjavur district of South India is a small hamlet; it is small in size, but has great sanctity hallowed by the memory of the three composers, the *Trimoorty*, of Carnatic music. In this village lived one Girija Kavi, a poet-composer attached to the Court of Tanjavur. His daughter and wife of Kakarla Ramabrahmam, Seetamma (Santamma?), gave birth to a son on *Sarvaji, Chaitra 27th Soma, Sukla Saptami, Pushya* (4th May 1767). According to another tradition the year of his birth was 1759. The boy was named Tyagaraja, after Lord Tyagaraja, the presiding deity of Tiruvarur. In one of his songs Tyagaraja sings. *"Seetamma Mayamma Sri Ramudu Ma tandri"*—Seeta is my mother and Sri Rama my father—perhaps with a double meaning.

Ramabrahmam shifted to Tiruvayyaru, leaving Tiruvarur. The king of Tanjavur had gifted a house to him in this village and here Tyagaraja not only spent the major part of his life but also attained *samadhi*. Tiruvayyaru, on the bank of the Kaveri and known as *Panchnada kshetra,* was the abode of saints, poets and musicians; and of this place Tyagayya sings,"... the *Panchanada kshetra* in the beautiful Chola country, nestling on the banks of the Kaveri over which blows the gentle zephyr where holy brahmins chant the Vedas...a town to be coveted even by Lord Siva".

Tyagabrahmam married, at the age of eighteen, a girl called Parvati who died without leaving any children. He then married her sister, Kanakamba. A daughter, Seetalakshmi, was born to them and she was given in marriage to Kuppuswami. They begot a boy who was named Tyagaraja (Panchapakesa?) who died issueless; thus came to an end the direct lineage of the composer.

Born and bred in a highly cultured family. Tyagaraja was a profound scholar and poet. He studied Sanskrit, astrology and was, of course, well versed in his mother tongue, Telugu. Besides, he was a highly trained musician, having been the disciple of Sonthi Venkataramanayya, one of the foremost singers of the day. His genius is evident in every song of his; but his immortal *Pancha ratna kritis* (the five gems) reveal the mastery he had over musical technique. Apart from thousands of songs of *kriti* type, he composed *Utsava sampradaya keertanas* and *Divya nama sankeertanas* which are sung in devotional congregations. He has also created two operas; *Prahlada Bhakti Vijayam* and *Nauka Charitram*. While there are a number of songs in Sanskrit, the majority of them, including the operas, are in Telugu.

One can speak of Tyagabrahmam's music only in superlatives and even these adjectives are pitifully inadequate to convey the exquisite beauty of his art. There is no hitch, there is no unwanted phrase, there is no laboured juxtaposition of word, music and feeling. To him music was so creative that he could not be bound in mere traditional grammar. He saw the potentiality in new melodies and from them gave forms to *ragas* like *Kharaharapriya, Harikambhoji* and *Devagandhari*; atleast he must have breathed life into such simple tunes to make them into *ragas*, if not produced them *de novo*. The rhythms used by him are also simple and are generally confined to *talas* such as *Adi, Triputa*, and *Roopaka*. Complex temporal and melodic patterns would not have expressed the lyricism of his mystic adoration. A beautiful elaboration introduced by him was the *sangati* as a built-in part of his *kriti*. These melodic variations convey so many shades of the main mood that all the finer nuances of text and music find expanded expression. It need not be offered as an excuse, but it is a fact that he was also as much capable of technical musicality as any learned grammarian. Tyagaraja's "five gems" in *ragas Nata, Gaula, Arabhi, Varali* and *Sri,* his songs in slower tempos and his famous *kriti, Mariyada kadayya* in *Bhairavi* wherein he effortlessly, brings in a shade of *Yaman Kalyan*—all these and many more show a mastery of design and structure very much beyond the ordinary.

Tyagaraja's literary genius was as great as his musical genius. His command over Telugu and Sanskrit lent not only an erudite dignity to his songs but gave a rare felicity and homeliness to his diction. He drives home great truths with unerring aim but with extreme simplicity of smile. "What does it matter whether the fool, who does not, gain *punya* (religious merit) when opportunity presents itself, lives or is dead"..... Of what avail is it whether blind eyes, however large, are open or closed?". Again, "The fault or goodness is not yours, Lord! It is mine. (Why blame Thee.) If one's daughter is unable to bear the labour-pains, why blame the son-in-law?".

Spiritually he was one of the rare souls who gave up everything except *bhakti* and cared for nothing else beyond the Grace of God. The early influences on his life make this trend more pronounced. The *Bhagavata of* Bammera Potana, the mystic poet of Andhra, was for him a book of daily *parayana* (recitation). Indeed there is a close parallel between the thoughts and loves of these two. The *devaranamas* of Purandaradasa were fed to him as if they were his mother's milk. Such early environment led to a positive direction by initiation into yoga. It is supposed that he was given the *Rama Taraka Mantra* by one *sanyasi*, Sri Ramakrishnananda. Tyagaraja's father's fellow scholar and a *yogi*, Sri Upanishad Brahmendra of Kanchipuram also exerted a great influence on him. So also the works and personality of Narayana Teertha, the author of *Krishnaleela Tarangini*, had considerable effect on the musician.

The only things that mattered to Tyagayya were music and *bhakti*—they were synonymous. "Is there a sacred path than music and *bhakti*?" . "O Mind, salute the gods of the seven notes". "The knowledge of music, O Mind, leads to bliss of Union with the Lord". Music was to him the meditation on the Primordial Sound: "I bow to Sankara, the embodiment of *Nada*, with my body and mind. To Him, the essence of blissful *Samaveda*, the best of the Vedas, I bow. To Him who delights in the seven *swaras* born of His five faces I bow".

Tyagaraja was a great *bhakta;* the only meaningful act for him was complete surrender to Him whom he called Rama. In the song *Ika gavalasina*, he sings, "What more do you want, O Mind! Why are you not happy? When the Lord of the Universe has rested in your heart—what more do you want, O mind?".

There was not a moment of his life which was not filled with Rama. His songs sing of Him who was a friend, a master, a father—anything he could conceive of. Hearing of Rama's name was to Tyagaraja like "obtaining a large kingdom". And how could he desist from singing His praises— "Is there any bliss greater than this: to dance, to sing and to pray for His presence." "Did not the Lord incarnate wish to wear the garland of *ragas* woven by Tyagaraja?".

The worship of His feet (*padasevana*) was a privilege; but to worship His sandals (*paduka*) was indeed a fortune. "Rama, clear my doubt. Are your holy feet worshipped by Narada, great or Your sandals? The sages who worshipped Your feet became equal to You; but Bharata worshipped Your sandals and got Your very self". Day in and day out His worship became a matter of daily living to Tyagaraja. He sang songs to wake the Lord, to bathe Him, to feed Him, to please Him and to put Him to bed— "You are tired after wandering in the forest and conquering Ravana; rest in the lotus of Tyagaraja's heart". Of course, being close to Rama he could chide Him. "If you present Yourself before me, what wealth will You lose? Why this intractability?".

The word Rama (RA-MA) was to him a Numen that transcended all names. It would be more than absurd to attribute any sectarian leanings in Tyagaraja. He sings, "As what did they define You? How did they worship You?—as Siva, as Madhava, as Brahma born of Lotus or as Parabrahma, the Trans–Godhead? It prostrate myself before those who know the secret of MA as the life of *Siva-mantra* and RA as the life of *Narayana-mantra*".

This complete surrender naturally made him live a life of detachment, though he was a house holder. The first and foremost result was that he refused to earn a livelihood. He had a house to live in and that was enough shelter. For food, every morning he would go round the village asking for alms—*unchaviritti*; as it is called; and he would not gather even alms more than his daily need.

A life which steadfastly was uncompromising was not at all to the liking of his elder brother, Japesa, to put it mildly. Japesa fondly hoped that the great art and learning of his younger brother could be put to pecuniary uses, which the saint would not agree to. In desperation, the brother not only partitioned the ancestral house but went to the extent of throwing the Rama idol which Tyagayya worshipped, into the river. The sorrow of the devotee cannot even be imagined. Many a song he sang begging the Lord to come back to him. In a dream he was told where to find the idol and his life became full.

Honour and wealth could have been his, if only he had asked for them, but he would not ask. He spurned an invitation of the King and sang, "Is wealth (*nidhi*) the source of happiness or is the proximity (*sannidhi*) of Rama?"

Tyagabrahma undertook an extensive pilgrimage of the sacred places of South India. Wherever he went he sang on the deity of the place. There is the famous incident of his visit to the Venkateshwara temple at Tirupati. He goes into the temple to have *darsan* (vision) of the Lord; but the entrance of the *sanctum sanctorum* is covered with a curtain which prevents him from seeing the idol. The priests refuse to part the curtain. In great sorrow he sings, "Will you not remove the curtain?".... and characteristically adds, "The curtain of vanity and jealousy in my mind. The curtain miraculously slides aside by itself and he is face to face with Him.

So much sincerity and surrender drew the ire of people around him and he could not stand their hypocrisy either. He speaks out bluntly about their pretences. "One who does not think of devotion to God, however learned, will be a slave of the senses and not be free from coveting others' women and wealth". "O Siva, is it possible for me to have your *darsan*? I have seen the spires, the pillars, the idols, the temple dancers, the rows of lights and made the due circumambulations. My mind has turned towards things external. But it is no child's play to instal Your glorious form in the lotus of my heart!" Again, "Of what use is the possession of scholarship, in *purana, agama, shastra, veda* and the doing of *japa* to a deceitful mind? It is like dressing a corpse with a lace turban and precious jewels. Oh, give me the alms of highest (*satvika*) devotion".

Tyagabrahma took *sanyas* towards the end of his life and attained *samadhi* on *Pusya Bahula Panchami* in *Prabhava* (6th January, 1847). There is a poignancy about his absorption into the Godhead. He says in one of the most moving songs. "Unerringly I saw Sri Rama installed on the hill... Thrilled with ecstasy, with tears of joy, I tried to speak. He promised to bless me in five days." And so it happened.

Muthuswami Dikshitar

Venkateswara Dikshitar and his spouse, Bhageerathi, lived in Varinchipuram in South India in the beginning of the 18th century. To them was born a son, Ramaswami, in 1735. The Dikshitars, however, had to leave this town, for hordes of armies were invading the contiguous areas and life was becoming disturbed. The family, therefore, migrated to the far southern district of Tanjavur, to a village, Govindapuram, on the banks of the Kaveri. Venkateswara settled there and led a peaceful life. Sometimes in the middle of the century he and his wife, died, leaving Ramaswami an orphan.

Ramaswami seems to have had an aptitude for music even from his boyhood and it was but natural that he decided to take it as a profession. So he went to Veerabhadrayya, a well-known musician of Tanjavur, and studied with him. A high proficiency only in the practical art did not satisfy him; hence, to study the intricacies of musical theory he became the disciple of Venkata Vaidyanatha who was a follower of the traditions of Govinda Dikshita and Venkatamakhi, the eminent musicologists. Thus, well trained in theory and practice, Ramaswami returned to Govindapuram which he later left and began to live in Tiruvarur. He was a very successful professional, honoured by royal and feudal houses. It is said that he was a creator of *raga Hamsadhvani*, which, in later days, became very popular. The songs of Muthuswami, his son, in this *raga* have become standard and models for composition in it in Hindustani music also.

Ramaswami and his wife, Subbammal, had no children for a long time. On the advice of a *yogi* he worshipped the Goddess Balambika. For forty days he prayed at the temple of Vaidiswara, following the methods of *tantra*. One the last day She came to him in a dream and gave him a string of pearls (*muktahara*). Before the year was out, in 1775, Subbammal gave birth to a son. He was named Muthukumaraswami, later to become revered as Muthuswami Dikshitar. It was, perhaps, no accident that the name takes after Lord Kartikeya, the deity of Vaidiswara temple, for the star under which Muthuswami was born was of Lord Kartikeya. Even the word *muthu* is significantly meaningful—it means 'pearl', a reference to the pearl necklace gifted in the dream. Muthuswami sings of Balambika as his mother; "O Mind, pray to Balambika, the giver of boons.... She is the mother of Muthukumara". Besides Muthukumara, Ramaswami had three more children—two sons, Chinnaswami and Baluswami, and a daughter, Balambika.

Manali was a principality near Madras and its proprietor was one Muthukrishna Mudaliar, a well-known patron of the arts. During one of his visits to Tiruvarur he had an occasion to listen to Ramaswami's singing. Deeply moved by it, the Mudaliar took the singer to his place and made him a court-musician. Muthukrishna Mudalir and his son, Venkatakrishna, revered and honoured Ramaswami Dikshitar who is said to have composed a *raga malika* of 108 *ragas* and *talas* as a dedication to Venkatakrishna.

Muthuswami Dikshitar's life gets a turn from this period. Chidambaranatha Yogi was a man of great occultic attainments and a preceptor of Ramaswami. The saint was on a pilgrimage to Kasi (Varanasi) and on his way to the holy town, paid a visit to his disciple. Young Muthu and his brother were put to looking after the comforts of the holy man. The demeanour and character of the boy did not go unnoticed by the *yogi*. On the day of the *swami's* departure, the family paid obeisance at his feet for blessings, as is the Hindu custom. It was then that the *guru* made his momentous request, "Send Muthuswami with me as my disciple and let him keep me company in my sojourn." To Ramaswami this was no pleasant order, as the boy had been born after arduous penance. While he dared not disobey, neither could he gladly agree. Venkatakrishna Mudaliar, however, interceded and persuaded the father to send the son with the *sanyasi,* for where could one find a greater guru than Chidambara Yogi. No evil but only the highest good could come out of such a holy request. The youth, then, left Manali on a pilgrimage to Kasi, serving the master.

Life at Kasi for Muthuswami, was one of study and meditation. For about six years he lived and learned with the *yogi*, mastering Sanskrit literature and grammar, philosophy and *tantra yoga*. It is believed that he might have followed his *guru* to temples even at Kathmandu (Nepal) and Badrinath, the sacred abodes of Lord Siva. Finally, on the eve of his departure from Varanasi, he went to Chidambara Yogi to take leave of him. The master said to him, "Go and have a bath in the Holy Ganga, before you leave. You will be blessed." Accordingly, Dikshitar went to the river and, descending a few steps, dipped into the water. And a miracle happened. A *veena* with the words 'Rama' inscribed came to him from the waters. Marvelling beyond measure, he took it to the *guru* who blessed him saying, "This is a divine gift. You will be a master of the *veena*. Muthuswami left Kasi for his home. This lute is said to be preserved to this day at the residence of his brother, Baluswami's descendents.

Though married early, to two wives, Muthuswami was by nature a wanderer in the spiritual path and visiting sacred places and worshipping at shrines there was, for him, an important part of religious life. So, not long after he returned home, he was again out on perigrinations. Leaving Manali he went his way to Tiruttani where Lord Subramania, his personal Godhead, was installed. Immersed in contemplation, he had a vision of the Lord and there he composed the *Tiruttani Kritis* with the signature *Guru Guha*. He sang, "Think of *Guru Guha* and cast off all agonies of mind." In another song he exclaims, "I am the servant of *Guru Guha*; nay, I am *Guru Guha*". From Tiruttani he went to Tirupati and Kalahasti, and returned to Manali. But he became restless and was off on a pilgrimage to Kanchipuram, presided over by Goddess Kamakshi. Actually he, along with his family, shifted to this town from Manali. Here he wrote many a song on Kamakshi and other deities; and while in that town he came into contact with Upanishad Brahmendra, the philosopher-*yogi* and studied with him vedantic philosophy. His wanderings did not cease there. Muthuswami visited Tiruvarur, Thanjavur and various other places.

Finally we find him in Ettiyapuram. His travel to this town has an interesting sidelight. While at a hamlet called Sattur, he heard from a few brahmins that the Raja of Ettiyapuram was celebrating the wedding of his court musician. Some curiosity prompted him to ask the musician's name. And the answer he got was a joyful one; the bridegroom was none other than Baluswami, his younger brother. Eager and thrilled he joined the party and proceeded to Ettiyapuram. It was indeed a happy meeting of the brothers, separated for years. At the request of the king he settled there and became his *guru*. It was here that he passed away in 1834.

The personality of Muthuswami has an enormous dignity, like his music. Shunning wealth, he aspired for nothing but the blessings of his chosen

Godhead. Worship, particularly of a *Tantric* kind, study and music were everything for him. This is reflected in his music through and through. While there is no emotional ebullience in the poetry of his songs, unlike Tyagaraja's, one can even say that every one of these is a *mantra*.

His musical training was mainly under his father, Ramaswami Dikshitar and he had become highly proficient in it even in his childhood. But there are a few aspects of his art which are of great importance. One, his acquaintance with the violin, a Western instrument. Ramaswami and his son had occasion to visit Madras, particularly Fort St. George which was the seat of the British Governments then. Here they got many opportunities to listen to Western bands, in which Ramaswami must have heard the violin. He learnt the instrument and adapted it to Carnatic music and accompanied singers on it. Though Muthuswami played *veena*, Vadivelu, a disciple of his became an adept at handling the violin and introduced it at the court of Maharaja Swati Tirunal of Travancore. From then on it has become accepted as a premier instrument in the South. Besides, Dikshitar has written about fifty songs based on English tunes, one even modelled on "God Save the King". These, of course, cannot be taken very seriously. Secondly, his stay at Kasi brought him into close touch with North Indian music. He seems to have imbibed the spirit and technique of that system. Many melodic phrases he uses suggest Hindustani musical progressions. He has composed *kritis* in *ragas* like *Brindavani Sarang, Hamir Kalyani* (very similar to *Kedar* of the North) and so on. Thirdly, his being a *veena* player has coloured his style. The *gamakas* he employs, the range of pitch that his songs cover, leaps and bounds in all the octaves. All these are very telling influences of the instrument.

Dikshitar was not a very prolific composer; there are several hundreds of songs mainly *kritis*, besides a few *raga-malikas*. They are in common and rare *ragas,* but the versatility and imagination in every one of them is extraordinarily profound. In uncommon *ragas* such as *Saranga Nata, Kumudakriya* and *Amritavarshini* we have only his pieces as references. Of the better known are his *Tirtuttani kritis, Navavarana kritis* and *Navagraha kritis*. An interesting musical progression he generally uses is the doubling of tempo. That is, a couple of cycles of the opening of the *pallavi* and/or *anupallavi* will move in a given tempo. The rest of the section is completed by the text and music being arranged at double this speed. Case inflection of words (*vibhakti*) is another of his curious usages. A phrase is so constructed that it can be split without losing its meaningfulness. A well-known example is *"Tyagaraja Yoga Vaibhavam"* in *raga Anandabhairavi*. This set of words can be divided into sections such as *raja yoga vaibhavam, yoga vaibhavam, vaibhavam* and *bhavam*.

There is a saying in South India that the music of Tyagaraja is like a grape—the moment you put it in your mouth, it dissolves and is sweet; that of Syama Sastry is like a banana—one has to peel the skin to eat it. But the art of Dikshitar is like a coconut; if you want to taste the milk inside, you will have to break the hard outer shell.

Swati Tirunal

The Royal House of Kerala is renowned for its great warriors, administrators and patrons of art. Besides, some of them have been themselves artists of outstanding merit. A family of learning and piety, the *rajas* of Travancore have dedicated themselves and the welfare of their state to Lord Padmanabha who presides over the destinies of this people.

Of this House there was one Balarama Varma, a very learned and popular king, who died issueless. He was the author of *Balarama Bharatam,* a highly respected work. After the demise of Raja Balarama Varma, his sister, Gouri Lakshmi Bai, became the ruler of the state. She had two sons. The elder one was born on April 13, 1813 under the star Swati. So, according to tradition, the prince was named Swati Tirunal Rama Varma. When two years old, he lost his mother and from then on, along with his brother, came under the guardianship of their aunt (mother's sister), Gouri Parvati Bai. Rama Varma, at the age of sixteen, was annointed the Maharaja of Travancore.

The boy must have been very precocious indeed. For he soon became well versed in nearly thirteen languages including Sanskrit, Malayalam, Telugu, Kannada, Marathi, Hindi and English. The prince was proficient enough to write poems in these tongues. He was also good at painting, sculpture and other arts. Swati Tirunal, however, is best known for his compositions and patronage of musicians. He has penned a number of poetic works such as *Padmanabha Satakam, Kuchelopakhyanam* and *Ajamilopakhyanam*, the last two being specially meant for *Harikatha Kalakshepam* (religious discourse). In the Carnatic style he has a number of *kritis, varnams, padams* and *javalis* to his credit. His genius did not restrict itself to South Indian music; but he has to his credit *dhrupads, kheyals, thumris* and so on. Rama Varma used as his signature, 'Padmanabha' or some other variation of this name, as a dedication to the Presiding God of Travancore.

Besides being a musician himself, he was one of the most generous patrons of art of his day and had in his court musicians and scholars of both South and North. Of these the better known ones were Ravivarman Tampi, Koli Tampiran, Punjab Sulemen, Allauddin, Meruswami, Vadivelu (the

violinist and disciple of Muthuswami Dikshitar) and his brothers, Kannayya
Bhagavatar (the disciple of Tyagaraja) and many others. It was Vadivelu
who had made the violin recognized as an instrument of great potentialities
in Carnatic music, and in appreciation of his merits, Maharaja Swati Tirunal
had gifted him a violin of ivory. It is said that the Maharaja had even sent a
musician to Tyagaraja with his songs for comments of the saint. Not only so,
he had also a strong desire to bring Tyagabrahamam to his court. It was a
delicate mission; so Vadivelu was chosen to convey the King's wishes to
Tyagaraja through Veena Kuppayyar, a student of the bard and friend of
Vadivelu. The violinist set forth and reached Tiruvayyaru, where he managed
to get acquainted with Tyagayya. He played many a composition of Swati
Tirunal to Tyagaraja. Pleased with the music, the saint blessed Vadivelu
and asked as to what he could do in return. This violinist broached the
subject gently, for he knew of Tyagaraja's aversion to kings and kingly
pleasures; "Maharaja Swati Tirunal will deem it an honour if you could
kindly agree to grace his court". The great man is said to have replied, "I
shall certainly meet him; but in the next world, as the deities of our worship
are the same". The *raja* and the recluse never met in this world! Tirunal
was not free enough to go to Thiruvayyaru and Tyagaraja had no intentions
of leaving it.

Swati Tirunal Rama Varma passed away on December 25, 1846

Rabindranath Tagore

No account of Indian music and its modern cultural impact is complete
without a study of Rabindranath. No other personality exercised so great
an influence on and elicited so unreserved adulation from the world of art
as he did. There is no field of culture where Tagore's presence has not been
felt; education, literature, painting, dance, drama and music. Creative
personalities—young and old— in all these areas turned to him for inspiration
and guidance.

Rabindranath belonged to a family of Bengali brahmins who had come
to settle in Govindpur, from Jessore. Govindpur was the area where now
stands Fort William in Calcutta. The family began to be called the *Thakurs,*
and Tagore is an Anglicised corruption of this word. The East India Company
was then a major money spinner as well as a great 'cultural' attraction to
the *babus.* One Jayram Thakur came under the benevolent umbrella of this
British trading company and soon was a well-to-do man. His great grandson
was Dwarakanath Thakur who added immensely to the family fortunes and
grew to be a big landlord. Though the Thakurs became Rajas and one of the
leaders of elite fashions, 'Prince' Dwarakanath, soon was drawn towards
the social revolutionary, Raja Ram Mohan Roy. From here this branch of the

Thakur family takes a new turn in life. Dwarakanath's son was Devendranath, a man of sterling honesty and spiritual unfoldment. He was held in high esteem not only by the members of his religious faith—the Adi Brahma Samaj—but by orthodox Hindus as well, and was spoken of as the Maharishi, the great sage. Rabindranath was the fourteenth child of Devendranath and was born on May 7, 1861.

Rabi never seemed to have taken well to formal schooling. The Oriental Seminary, the Bengal Academy and St. Xavier's School were of no interest to the young boy who was more at home in Santiniketan, the quiet grove which his father had acquired in 1863. He had, however, private tutors at home and from the Maharishi he got instructions in Sanskrit, English and astronomy. Formal education, perhaps, would have stultified the boy's genius which began to blossom out even in his teens when he wrote the famous Vaishnava lyrics under the pen-name Bhanu Sinha Thakur. This created a sensation; for, it is said, that his style and content were so closely imitative of poets like Vidyapati that researchers—not knowing the real 'Bhanu' discussed, with much fervour and erudition, the historical antecedents of author "Bhanu Sinha!"

By the age of twenty Rabindranath's genius found definite outlets; in 1881 his musical drama, *Balmiki Pratibha,* was written and put on the stage, the author himself taking the role of Valmiki. This musical play is significant, as here, for the first time, he bodily transported English and Irish melodies. As he admits, this was an interesting experiment in "loosening the chains of melodic forms", inspired by his visit to England.

Sandhya Sangeet (Songs of Evening) written when Tagore was barely twenty elicited a warm tribute from the older poet Bankim Chandra. He had also completed the verse-drama, *Bhagna Hridaya* (Broken Heart), the novel, *Thakuranir Hat* (The Young Queen's Market) and the musical drama, *Kal Mrigaya* (The Fatal Hunt). As the young writer matured, essays, novels, dramas, songs and philosophical reflections—all too numerous to mention— flowed from his pen. The world will, however, remember at least his *Mayar Khela, Bisarjan, Manasi, Ksudit Pasan, Gora, Nauka dubi, Gitanjali, Chitrangada* and *Chandalika*. And the world also recognized his greatness by awarding him the Nobel Prize for Literature in 1913.

Tagore was caught, like almost every other Indian of that time, in the nationalistic upsurge. But he could not draw himself into the whirlpool to Sri Aurobindo or Mahatma Gandhi. While, in later life, Sri Aurobindo completely isolated himself from such struggle, Rabindranath also could sense that it might take unhealthy directions. He, therefore, kept a distance, though he did write 'nationalistic' essays and songs. The various tours abroad (nearly eleven of them) undertaken by him, gave him a deeper insight into the struggle of the human soul for liberty and he saw that the Indian strife for freedom was only one instance of this larger striving of the race of men. Every 'patriotic' song or poem of his is, hence, a cry of the soul of a man in anguish.

Socially, his most meaningful contribution was the *Viswabharti*—the Universal seat of Learning—at Santiniketan, the Abode of Peace. Here he attempted to build a haven of his vision; a place where "the mind is without fear and the head is held high." It was to be a place which knew no emotional, social, religious or political inhibitions and barriers. Students, scholars, saints, and political upstarts—all found there an air clean to breathe. Viswabharati was not 'International' for it was never 'National'.

The remarkable sojourn of the poet on this earth came to an end on August 7, 1941. The most wonderous beauty of Rabindranath's life was that it was bereft of obvious melodrama, at least externally. There is not the agony of Tyagaraja, neither is there the sudden epiphany of Purandaradasa. There is no occultic initiation of Muthuswami Dikshitar. This soul seems to have been born an angel, lived like an angel and passed over like an angel. His personal life was not one of extreme turmoil, though the first decade of this century was a sad one for him—he lost his wife, his father and two children. Even this bereavement was for him a play of the Lord; often he has written in the vein, "This game of defeat and victory is life's delusion; from childhood, at each step, clings this spectre, filled with sorrow's mockery."

Tagore, as a musician, has a unique niche. He cannot be considered an orthodox virtuose, though he had sound technical knowledge. Rabindranath was not a lax, undisciplined adventurer, for his songs are well chiselled and finely proportioned in form and content. He accepted bondage, not rigidity, freedom but not licence. A soul of a *gandharva*, he could not be bound and limited by exercises in musical scale; therefore, as with academic education, he never subjected himself to the routine of training. His musical education consisted in *being* musical. His home was, from his childhood, a resort for musicians; *jatra* players, *ustads, pandits and* "an unknown musician (who) stayed for a few days just as he chose". The early childhood of the composer was filled with the "commonest kind of Bengali folk songs" which "no present day musician, whether famous or obscure, would have consented to touch." When he was a little older "a very great musician called Jadu Bhatta came and stayed in the house. He made one big mistake in being determined to teach me music, and consequently no teaching took place." Among well known musicians who visited Rabindranath's house were Moula Baksh, Vishnuram

Chakravarty, Radhika Goswami and Srikantha Sinha. The most effective teacher was Rabindranath's elder brother, Jyotindranath, "My brother, Jyotindranath, was engaged the livelong day at his piano, refashioning the classic melodic forms at his pleasure... we could plainly hear the tunes speak to us...." Young Rabi himself practised his songs with the *tambura* on his shoulder, for "the harmonium, that bane of Indian music, was then not in vogue" and he did not subject himself to the "slavery of the keyboard". Fortunately, even after his death, this instrument has been a taboo in his university, Viswabharati.

In spite of a lack of any form of drilling—perhaps, because of it— Rabindranath's music is both technically and aesthetically of a very high order. He not only created songs with words and music of his own, but wrote poems for others' music and gave music to others' poems. The compositional form included *dhrupad, thumri* and *tappa* though the majority were just songs. Nevertheless, they show sectional divisions of *asthayi* and *antara*. He drew extensively from Bengali folk tunes such as *sari, baul* and *keertan*. The composer was, in spirit, himself a *baul,* a mystic wanderer intoxicated with godly love. His visits abroad brought him close to foreign music and he did not hesitate to transplant it into his own songs. It may be of interest to know of his reactions to European music: "when I was in Brighton, I once went to hear some Prima Donna.... Never before had I came across such an extraordinary command over the voice. Even our best singers cannot hide their sense of effort; nor are they ashamed to bring out as best as they can, top notes or bass notes beyond their proper register. In our country the understanding portion of the audience think no harm in keeping the performance up to standard by dint of their own imagination. For the same reason they do not mind any harshness of voice or uncouthness of gesture in the exponent of a perfectly formed melody,.... they seem sometimes to be of the opinion that such minor external defects serve better to set off the internal perfection of the composition—as with the outward poverty of the Great Ascetic, Mahadeva, whose divinity shines forth naked."

"This feeling seems entirely wanting in Europe. There, the outward embellishment must be perfect in every detail, and the least defect stands shamed and unable to face the public gaze. In our musical gatherings nothing is thought of spending half an hour in tuning up the *Tampuras*, of hammering into tune the drums, little and big. In Europe such duties are performed beforehand, behind the scenes, for all that comes in front must be faultless.... In our country a correct and artistic exposition of the melody is the object of culture and with it they perform impossibilities. In our country the virtuoso is satisfied if he has heard the song; in Europe, they go to hear the singer."

"European music seems to be intertwined with its material life, so that the text of its songs may be as various as that of life itself. If we attempt to put our tunes to the same variety of use they tend to lose their significance, and become ludicrous, for our melodies transcend the barriers of everyday life, and only thus can they carry us so deep into Pity, so high into Aloofness, their function being to reveal a picture of the inmost inexpressible depths of our being, mysterious and impenetrable, where the devotee may find his hermitage ready, or even the epicurean his bower, but where there is no room for the busy man of the world."

About European music he further says, "It seemed to me so romantic. It is somewhat difficult to analyse what I mean by that word. What I would refer to is the aspect of variety of abundance, of the waves on the sea of life, of the ever-changing light and shade on their ceaseless undulations."

Of *ragas* he used many of the common ones, the frequent being *Bhairavi, Khamaj, Pilu, Malhar* and *Bihag*. Specially in *Bhairavi* he created unpredictably different moods. But he could not limit himself to *ragas* of the orthodox repertoire; so he produced new combinations like *Asavari-Bhairavi, Darbari-Todi-Bhairavi, Bhairav-Bhairavi, Multani-Bhimpalasi* and so on. New *talas* like *sasthi* (2+4), *navami* (5+4 or 3+2+2+2), *jhampak* (3+2+3+2) and *rupakada* (3+2+3+2) were his contributions.

Besides the musical quality *per se* his songs have an inseparable fusion of the moods of words and tunes. Of this, Rabindranath says, "The art of vocal music has its own special functions and features. And when it happens to be set to words, the latter must not presume too much on their opportunity and seek to supersede the melody of which they are but the vehicle. The song being great in its own wealth, why should it wait upon the words? Rather does it begin where more words fail. Its power lies in the region of the inexpressible, it tells us what the words cannot."

"So the less a song is burdened with words, the better. In the classic style of Hindustani the words are of no account, and leave the melody to make its appeal in its own way. Vocal music reaches its perfection when the melodic form is allowed to develop freely, and carry our consciousness with it to its own wonderful plane. In Bengal, however, the words have always asserted themselves, so that our provincial song has failed to develop her full musical capabilities, and has remained content as the handmaiden of her sister art of poetry. From the old Vaishnava songs down to those of Nidhi Babu (Ramnidhi Gupta, 19th cent.) she has displayed her charms from the background. But as in our country the wife rules her husband through acknowledging her dependence, so our music, though professedly in attendance, only ends by dominating the song".

A mystic of the same madness as Sri Chaitanya and Sri Ramakrishna, Rabindranath saw the creation as the Lover playing with his Beloved. All the world and all this life was a Song of Union and Separation, of Joy and Pain, of Victory and Defeat.

"I know not how thou singest, my master! I ever listen in silent amazement."

"The light of thy music illumines the World. The life-breath of thy music runs from sky to sky. The holy stream of thy music breaks through all stony obstacles and rushes on.

"My heart longs to join in thy song, but vainly struggles for a voice. I would speak, but speech breaks not into song, and I cry out baffled. Ah, thou hast made my heart captive in the endless meshes of thy music, my master!"

SUGGESTED FURTHER READING

Ashton, R. (E.d), *Music: East and West,* (Indian Council for Cultural Relations, New Delhi, (1966). A comparative study of Indian and Western music.

Athavale, V.R., *Pandit Vishnu Digambar*, (National Book Trust, New Delhi, 1967), Biography.

Barua, H., *Folk Songs of India*, (Indian Council for Cultural Relations, New Delhi. 1963). Descriptive collection of texts of folk songs.

Bhattacharya, S. *Ethnamusicology and India,* (Indian Publ., Calcutta, 1968). Introduces folk and tribal music.

Coomaraswami, A., *The Dance of Shiva,* (Asia, Bombay), Aesthetics.

Danielou, A., *The Ragas of North Indian Music,* (Munshi Ram Manoharlal, Delhi). Notations (staff) of Hindustani ragas.

Danielou, A., *Northern Indian Music,* (Halcyon, London, 1984) 2 vols. Theory and History, notations (staff).

Danielou, A., *Introduction to the Study of Musical Scales,* (India Society, London. 1954). Detailed study of musical scales of the world.

Day, C.R., *Music & Musical Instruments of Southern India & the Decean,* (B.R. Publ., Repost. 1974).

Deva, B.C., *Music of India: Scientific Study,* (Munshi Ram, Manoharlal, Delhi-1980). Physics and Psychology.

Deva, B.C., *Music,* (Indian Council for Cultural Relations, Delhi, 1974). General.

Deva, B.C., *Musical Instruments,* (National Book Trust, Delhi, 1978). Introductory.

Deva, B.C. & Kuckertz, Jr. Bharud, *Vaghya-Murali and the Daffgan of the Deccan,* (Katzbichler West Germany). Folk music.

Fox Strangways, A.H., *The Music of Hindustan,* (Oxford, 1965) Detailed General.

Gangoly. O.C., *Ragas and Raginis,* (Nalanda, Bombay, 1948). Classification of *ragas* and iconography.

Ghosh, N., *Fundamentals of Raga and Tala with a new system of Notation,* (1968) Introductory General.

Goswami, O., *The Story of Indian Music.* (Asia, Bombay, 1957). General.

Jairaz Bhoy., N.A., *The Ragas of North Indian Music,* (Faber, 1971), Advanced Analysis.

Jones, W., and Willard, N.A., *Music of India,* (Sushil Gupta, Calcutta, Reprint, 1962). General.

Joshi. B., *Understanding Indian Music,* (Asia, 1963). Elementary.

Kaufmann, W., *The Ragas of North India,* (Oxford & IBH, 1968), Notations (staff) of Hindustani *Ragas.*

Kaufmann. W., *The Ragas of South India*, (Oxford & IBH, 1976).

Krishnaswamy, S., *Musical Instruments of India*. (Publications Divn., Govt., of Ind., New Delhi, 1967), Introductory.

Krishnaswamy, S.Y., *Thyagaraja*, (Longmans, 1968). Biography.

Misra, Sushila, *Music Profiles*, (Lucknow). Biographies.

Parmar, S., *Folk Music & Mass Media*, (Communication Publ. 1977).

Prajnananda, Swami, *A History of Indian Music*, (Anandadhara, Calcutta, 1965). Detailed study of muscial development.

Prajnananda, Swami, *A Historical Study of Indian Music*, (Ramakrishna Vedanta Math, Calcutta, 1963). Mainly North Indian.

Raghavan, V., *Great Integrators – the Saint Singers of India*, (I&B), Ministry, 1966).

Ramanujachari, C., *Spiritual Heritage of Tyagaraja*, (Ramakrishna Math Students Home, Madras, 1957). Texts and English translations of songs; with Introductory Thesis by V. Raghavan.

Ranade, G.H., *Hindustani Music*, (Poona). General.

Ratanjankar, S.N., *Pundit Bhatkhande*, (National Book Trust, 1967). Biography.

Ravi Shankar, *My Music and My Life*, (Vikas, 1968).

Ray, S., *Music of Eastern India*, (Firms KLM, 1973), Regional types.

Sambamoorthy, P., *South Indian Music*. Vols. 1-6, (Ind.. Mas. Pub. Hs.). Graded series.

Sambamoorthy, P., *Great Composers*. (Ind. Mus. Pb. Hs.).

Sambamoorthy P., *(1) Sruti Vadya, (2) Z. Laya Vadya*, (All Ind. Handicrafts Bd., New Delhi 1957). Folk and concert instruments, mainly their structures and uses.

Sambamoorthy, P., *Tyagaraja*, (Nat. Bk, Trust, New Delhi, 1967). Texts (English translations) of folk songs.

Satyarthi, D., *Meet my People*, (Chetana, Hyderabad, (1951), Texts (English translations) of folk songs.

Sitaramiah. V., *Purandaradasa*, (National Book Trust, 1967). Biography.

Subba Rao, T.V., *Studies in Indian Music*, (Asia, 1965). Collected essays on Karanatak Music.

Tagore, Rabindranath., *Anthology of One Hundred Songs*, in staff notation (Sangeet Natak Akademi, New Delhi).

Venkatarama Aiyar, T.L., *Muthuswami Dikshitar*, (Nat. Bk. Trust, New Delhi, 1968). Biography.

Vidya Shanker, *Syama Sastry*, (Nat. Bk. Trust, 1970). Biography.

JOURNALS

Journal of the Music Academy, Madras.

Sangeet Natak, Sangeet Natak Akademi, New Delhi.

Journal of the National Centre for the Performing Arts, Bombay.

Journal of the Musicological Society of India. Baroda.

DISCOGRAPHY

General

Introducing Indian Music (Demonstration Lectures), B. Joshi & A. Lobo	33 PIX	1001-1004

A Musical Anthology of the Orient-India.   BM301   2006-2007
With notes by Alain Danielou (*Rigveda, Samaveda,
Yajurveda, music of Bharata Natyam dance—alarippu,
jatisvaram, javali, padam, tillana, varnam, slokam,
Kathakali dance music*).UNESCO-Musicaphone.

Classical Indian Music. With notes by Narayana   PMAE   501-503
Menon. (*Veena*–K.S. Narayanaswami,
vocal–M.S. Subbulakshmi, *sitar*–Ravi Shankar,
sarod–Ali Akbar Khan, *shenai*–Bismillah Khan,
mridangam–Palghat Mani Iyer).
International Cultural Centre—Parolphone.

An Introduction to the Music of India.   ECLP   2363
Arranged by Jnan Prakash Ghosh.
(*Sarod*–Radhika Mohan Moitra,
sitar–Kalyani Roy,
Hindustani vocal-A. Kanan & Malavika Kanan).

UNESCO collection,
Modal Music. VI-8,
(South Indian *veena*)   6586   023

UNESCO collection Musical Sources   6586   009

UNESCO collection, North Indian Instrumental Music   6586   020

UNESCO collection Indian Music I and II   MB30L   2006-2007

HINDUSTANI

Vocal

Dhrupad, dhamar
N.M. & N.A. Dagar   *Darbari Kanada, &c*   EALP   1291

N.Z. & N.F. Dagar	*Jaijaivanti, &c*	EALP	1334
Rahimuddin Dagar	*Todi*	7EPE	1206
Faiyyaz Khan	*Des*	EALP	1365

Kheyal
Gwalior and related gharanas

Nissar Hussein Khan	*Lalit. & c*	ECSD	2498
Omkarnath Thakur	*Devgiri Bilaval &c*	33EC	3751
Omkarnath Thakur	*Desi Todi. &c*	33ECK	3252
Krishnarao S. Pandit	*Todi &c*	ECSD	2453
V.N. Patwardhan & N. Vyas	*Malgunji &c*	EALP	1314
D.V. Paluskar	*Lalit. &c*	EALP	1295

Agra gharana

Faiyyaz Khan	*Lalit, &c*	EALP	1292
Vilayat Hussain Khan	*Paraj, &c*	7EPE	1207
Sharafat Hussein Khan	*Anandi, &c*	ECSD	2495

Jaipur-Atroli gharana

Kesarbai Kerkar	*Lalit. &c*	EALP	1278
Kishori Amonkar	*Jaunpuri, &c*	ECLP	2326
Mallikarjun Mansur	*Jaunpuri, &c*	S/ECSD	2402

Patiala gharana

Bade Ghulam Ali Khan	*Goonkali, &c*	EALP	1258
Bade Ghulam Ali Khan	*Darbari Kanada, &c*	EALP	1265

Kirana gharana

Abdul Karim Khan	*Basant, &c*	33 ECX	3253
Abdul Karim Khan	*Bilaval, &c*	33 ECX	3251
Roshan Ara Begum	*Suddha Kalyan, &c*	CLP	1530
Hirabai Barodekar	*Multani, &c*	ECLP	2275
Bhimsen Joshi	*Lalit, &c*	ECLP	2264
-do-	*Pooriya, etc*	S/EASD	1513

Other schools

Amir Khan	*Marwa &c*	EALP	1253
do	*Hamsadhvani &c*	EASD	1357
Kamar Gandharva	*Sanjari, &c*	ECLP	2284
do	*Sri Kalyan, &c*	S/ECSD	2734
Jasraj	*Nat bhairav, &c*	ECLP	2325
Nazakat Ali & Salamat Ali	*Madhuvanti, &c*	EALP	1264

Tarana

Nissar Hussein Khan	*Jhinjihoti*	7EPE	1242

Nissar Hussain Khan	*Pooriya dhanasri*	7EPE	1202

Thumri, etc
Bade Ghulam Ali Khan		EBLP	1751
Barkat Ali Khan		EALP	1510
Begum Akhtar		ECLP	2374
Rosoolan Bai		SEDE	3301
Siddheswari Devi		SEDE	3304

Bhajans
Dilip Kumar Roy		EALP	1379
Narayanrao Vyas		7EPE	1357
Omkarnath Thakur		SEDE	3304
D.V. Paluskar		EALP	1263

Instrumental

Svaramandal
D.R. Parvatikar	*Bhairavi, &c*	ECLP	2301

Santoor
Shivkumar Sarma	*Lalit, &c*	ECLP	2346

Rudra Veena
Shivkumar			
Z.M. Dagar	*Todi, &c*	7EPE	1312

Sitar
Abdul Halim Jaffar Khan	*Jaijaiwanti &c*	33 ESX	4253
Imrat Hussain (*Surbahar*)	*Abhogi*	EASD	1358
Nikhil Banerjee	*Malkhaus, &c*	EALP	1318
Ravi Shankar	*Pooriya Dhanasri, &c*	EALP	1283
Vilayat Khan	*Saha Sughrai, &c*	ALP	1988

Sitar & Sarod
Ravi Shankar &			
Ali Akbar Khan	Sri, &c	EALP	1296

Sarod
Ali Akbar Khan	*Ahir Bhairav*	EASD	1391
Amjad Ali	*Des &c*	EALP	1316
Bahadur Khan	*Misra Pilu &c*	ECSD	2483
Sharan Rani	*Hemant, &c*	ECLP	2340

Vichitra veena
Ramesh Prem	*Miyam-ki Malhar*	7EPE	1328

Sarangi

Ramnarain	Patdeep &c	EALP	1312
Ramnarain	Gavati, &c	7EPE	1212
Sultan Khan	Lalit, &c	Poly	239280

Violin

Gajananrao Joshi	Bhimpalasi, &c	ECLP	2330
V.G. Jog	Jog, &c	EALP	1320

Flute

H.P. Chaurasia	Des. &c	ECSD	2388
Pannalal Ghosh	Marwa, &c	MOAE	5006
Vijayaraghava Rao	Abhogi, &c	ECLP	2357

Shehnai

Biamilla Khan	Basant &c	EALP	1306
Bismilla Khan	Asavari &c	EALP	1315
Bismilla Khan with Vilayat Khan	Gujari Todi, &c	ALP	2295
Siddharam Jadhav			
Sundri	Bhoop, &c	ECSD	2386

Pakhavaj and Tabla

Alla Rakha	Trital, &c	7EPI	1252
Chatur Lal	Trital	EALP	1312
Ahmedjan Thirakwa	Ektal, &c	7EPF	1254
Samta Prasad			
Thirakwa, Alkutakar	Jhaptal, &c	MOAE	5007
(tabla & pukhavaj)			

Jaltarang and Kastha tarang (Xylophone)

A. Mohile & Rijram	Bibhas	7EPE	1292

Modern Experiments

V. Balsara	Raga mood	ECLP	2366
Ravi Shankar	Improvizations	EALP	1288
Shankar & Jaikishan	Raga Jazz style	ECSD	2377
Shiv Kumar Sharma, *et al*	Call of the Valley	ECSD	2382
Timir Baran	Orchestrated ragas	ECLP	2261

Yehudi Menuhin,			
Ravi Shankar,			
Hephzibah Menuhin	Sonata and Indian	ASD	2294
Alla Rakha	ragas		

Tagore's music

Voice of Tagore		EALP	1256

Varshamangal songs		EALP	1317
Kanika Banerjee		EALP	1267
Suchitra Mitra		ECLP	2303
Chandalika (opera)		ECLP	2273
Mayur Khela (opera)		EALP	1269

CARNATIC

Vocal

Balamurali Krishna, M	*Compositions of Tyagaraja*	ECLP	2345
Balasubramaniam, G.N.	*Kalyani, &c*	ECLP	2323
	Harikambhoji, &c	S/33ES&	6408
John Higgins	*Bhairavi varnam, &c*	ECLP	2339
Mani Iyer, Madurai	*Raga Bhairasi-Thyagaraja*	33ESX	6004
Pattammal, D.K.	*Hari Kambhoji and other Ragas*	S/33ESK	6048
Ramanuja Iyengar, Ariyakkudi	*Kambhoji, &c*	SEDE	3630
Srinivasa Iyer, Semmangudi	*Arabhi, &c*	SHDE	3632
Subhalakshmi M.S.	*Composition of Tyagaraja, Swati Tirunal, Syama Sastry, Dikshitar, Purandaradasa and others*	MOAE	5001-5003
Subramaniam, Chittor	*Manirangu, &c*	SEDE	3642
Vaidyanatha Bhagavatar, Chembai	*Hamsadhvani*	33ESX	6009
Vasanthakumari, M.L.	*Varnam, Pallavi &c in Todi*	33ESX	6006
Vasanthakumar, M.L.	*Hindolam, &c*	33ESX	6001
	An Evening of Bharat Natyam	S/33ESX	6046

Instrumental

Veena

Classical Indian Music Introduced by Yehudi Menuhin (K.S. Narayanaswami, V.K. Narayana Menon, Palghat Raghu)		LXT	5600
Balachander, S.	*Melakarta melodies*	ECSD	2451-2
Balachander, S.	*Navaragamalika, &c*	ECLP	2305
Balachander, S.	*Varali: alapana, tanam and pallavi*	ECLP	2270
Chitti Babu	*Saurashtra, &c*	33ESX	6008

Emani Sankara Sastry	*Todi*	7EPE	1603
Nageswara Rao	*Subhapanttuvarali &c*	TAT	5001/25
	Eurasia		

Violin

Chowdiah T.	*Hamsadhvani, &c*	SEDI	3629
Gopalakrishnan., M.S.	*Saranga, &c*	7EPE	1636
Jayaraman, Lalgudi	*Saraswati, &c*	7EPE	1614
Jayaraman, L & Party			
(violin, flute, and *veena*)	*Mohana*	ECLP	2338
Krishnan, T.N.	*Keeravani*	SHDE	3609

Nagaswaram

Arunachalam. K.	*Kharaharpriya*	7EPE	61
Rajaratnam, T.K.	*Todi, alapana &c*	SEDE	3625
Sheikh Chinna Moula	*Kapi*	EDE	3627

Clarionet

Natarajan, A.K.C	*Abheri, &c*	7EPE	1609

Mridangam & other percussions

Gopalakrishnan, T.V. *et al*	*Adi talam*	SEDE	3621
(*mridangam, ghatam* and			
kanjeera)			
Ramabhadran. V	*Adi talam*	SEDE	3604

Index

Abhanga (s), 48,71,92

Abhinava raga manjari, 113

Abhirudagata, 25

Abhog, 41

Absolute pitch, 20

Absolute standard scales, 20

Adarang, 42,109

Adi Brahma Samaj, 135

Adi guru, 121

Adi, 77,126

Adigal, Ilango,26

Adiyappayya, Pacchimiriyam, 124

Aerophones, 57

Agama, 129

Aghouti, 102

Ahobala, 67

Ajamilopakhyanam, 133

Ajanta, 57,61,64

Akbar, Emperor, 40, 64, 81, 102, 103, 105, 106

Aksaras, 30-32,124

Alagu, 26,88

Alambana, 79

Alankara (s), 13,14,43,121

Alap, 38-43, 47,49,50,51,54,66,109

Algoza, 66

Ali Hussein, 111

Ali Khan, Nawab, 111,112

Alingya, 62

All India Music Conference (fifth) at Lucknow, 112

All India Radio (AIR), 94,96

Allauddin, 133

Alphabets: in music, 5; kinds of, 5

Amaravati, 61

Ananda bhairavi, 77

Andolana, 13

Anga (s), 20,21,30,31; of raga, 20; of tala, 30; of tetrachord,21,30,82

Anibaddha sangeeta, 38

Anibaddha, 38,40,46

Ankya, 62

Antara gandhara, 24

Antara, 17,24,41, 42,43,45,49,137

Anudatta, 23,86

Anudrutta (Aksara), 30,33

Anumandra sthayi, 17

Anupallavi, 45-48,132

Anuvadi, 12,15

Appar, 89,91

Arabhi, 126,146

Archika, 23; style, 76

Arohana, 9-11,15

Arunagirinathar, 48

Asavari-Bhairavi, 138

Ascent, 8,9,10,15,21,22,39

Astapadis, 46,100,101

Asthayi, 41,42,137

Asudhir, 101

Asvakranta, 25

Atitara sthayi, 17

Auduva, 8

Aurobindo, Sri, 92,135

Avanaddha vadya, 57,61,62

Avarohana,9,10,11

Avarta,29,30,34,35

B

Bada Kheyal, 42,43,47,54

Baghela, Ramchandra,105

Bahar **see** Ragas

Baiju, 101,102

Bakshu,101